Prepared
not
Scared

YOUR *GO-TO GUIDE* FOR STAYING SAFE IN AN UNSAFE WORLD

BILL STANTON

Copyright © 2019 by Galvanized Media, LLC

Distributed by Simon & Schuster

ISBN 9781940358369
Ebook ISBN 9781940358406

Printed in the United States of America on acid-free paper.

Design by J. Heroun

Dedicated to Frankie Parlato and Jack Maple,
who have left an indelible mark on all who knew and loved them.
Their fighting spirit lives on in this book.

CONTENTS

INTRODUCTION

 **HIS BOOK** may save your life.

Or the lives of those you care most about—your children, your parents, your spouse, an aunt or uncle.

Or even the lives of complete and utter strangers—fellow passengers on a plane, happenstance commuters on a train, a passing pedestrian, or other guests at a restaurant or—if you're a born-and-raised New Yorker like me—the local neighborhood bodega.

The point is not to scare you. If you've picked up this book, chances are you are all too aware of just how unsafe our world has become. Whether you are at home checking your social media accounts or abroad traveling for work or vacation, you quite simply are neither safe nor secure. Many of you reading this may have already experienced an attack on your own safety—from petty theft to sexual assault. Or, just by watching the nightly news, you've realized that the routine you take for granted could be gone in an instant.

Let's review a few sobering factoids. A person is robbed in America every two seconds. An aggravated assault takes place every forty-one seconds. An innocent person is murdered every thirty-four minutes. There's a rape every four minutes. A home is burglarized every fifteen seconds. Violent crime is showing signs of RISING—and violent crime even increased in 2015. And those are just crimes of malicious intent—what about building safety, street safety, car safety? What about broad-based attacks? And what about simple accidents?

From tragedies as shocking as mass, unpredictable shootings, to the common threat of our everyday internet use facilitating identity theft at never-before-seen rates, let's face it: You are under threat of attack every single day. I wrote this book to help you mitigate what I see as ever-growing threats.

Every victim, when they walked out their door on the morning that changed their life and brought them pain, never anticipated what would happen to them that day—and just maybe, they didn't know how to react or what to do at the moment their lives changed forever.

The fact is that in this day and age, you need to walk around prepared. You need to get into your car prepared. You need to enter your workplace prepared. You can't afford NOT to be prepared. We need a guidebook, a user's manual for making it through another day in this modern world—a world that can be terrifying.

For some of you, putting the basics of this book into practice will mean that that moment will never come for you. For others, you can follow every rule to the letter and malicious intent or a tragic accident will still befall you. The question is: Will you be able to rise to the challenge and do everything you can when danger strikes?

After you read this guide, you will walk through life prepared, not scared. This book identifies where you're at risk—and then tells you how to best mitigate those risks with advice from the top experts in the field. I know of no other effort to bring together the insights and tips of so many experts. The book you hold in your hands today provides you with cutting-edge advice for a broad range of scenarios—as a reference you can use over and over again.

WHY THIS BOOK, WHY NOW

**WROTE THIS BOOK** because, over the course of a three-decade career, I've seen too much not to write it.

I have cared about safety and security for about as long as I can remember. Since my childhood, I have been on the path to police officer, and ultimately security expert. Not because I can claim descent from a long line of law enforcement officers. My family origins are strictly civilian. My father was an ironworker and a cabdriver, and my mother was a secretary. But growing up with both parents working, whenever they weren't sleeping, I was mostly raised by Grandma and Grandpa, and my babysitters were TV shows and movie theaters—specifically, John Wayne, Charles Bronson, and Robert Conrad, along with *The Wild Wild West*, *Baretta*, and *Magnum PI*. The die was cast—with those protagonists as my role models, I wouldn't rest until I was a police officer.

Obsessed with protecting and defending, I started out by volunteering for the PS 175 Safety Patrol. From New York City's standpoint, this meant a free crossing guard and doorman at the start of every school day. For me, it meant my first badge—which I believe my proud mother still has to this day.

Fast-forward, and after taking multiple police exams, my childhood ambition came true—at the ripe old age of twenty years and three days, I stood with my right hand raised, took the oath to protect and serve, and became a New York City cop. But as the excitement of initiation faded, I sensed that I had a long way to go. Most obvious to me at that time was that, although I had earned the badge, I could not buy a beer without risk of getting arrested myself.

They assigned me to the Fortieth Precinct. If you're not familiar, let me paint a picture. At the time, the Four-O sat at 138th Street and Alexander Avenue in the South Bronx. Yeah, that South Bronx. My Alcatraz. Everything you've heard about it is true. It ranked among the highest crime areas in the city. Calling it a war zone would be a compliment. I joke, but for a rookie fresh on the street, without guidance or mentorship, every day brought risks on a big platter. You name it, it was worse. Anything could happen in the line of duty. But here's the thing, and I didn't know this at the time: Back in the 1980s, if you were assigned to the Fortieth as a young "boot," that meant you had no connections or had screwed up something serious. Since I hadn't had a chance to step on anyone's toes yet, I'd prefer to think it was the latter. And it was true, I had zero connections. No NYPD friends or family to look out for me.

That precinct didn't disappoint. It was my trial by fire. I saw horrendous things. But I also saw great things—tremendous acts of bravery, kindness, and heroism. I met some of the finest people walking the earth. Decades later, I'm still close with many of my brother and sister officers from the Four-O. And at the time, as my experience grew and I started drying out behind the ears, my drive to protect the weak grew. I was a cop. I could do this.

One officer in particular helped show me the good path forward. I was lucky. Not everyone gets the benefit of partnering with a thirty-year veteran of the force when they're starting out. Sergeant Al Parlato was Obi-Wan Kenobi to my Luke Skywalker. He began as my Alcatraz mentor and remains my best friend and peer. Bronx born and raised, just like me, he served in the Army and then gave three decades to hard police work. He never left the streets to take a cushier, safer post. Much of what I know about the nuances of law enforcement, discretion, and common sense (which is a rarer commodity than you think), I learned from him. He taught me to conduct myself as an officer and, just as important, a gentleman.

So there I am, three years in, sitting side by side with Al in a radio car. It's a routine night in March. We drove around so Al could check up on the other cops out on foot patrol. That's what a good sergeant does. And then, boom, out of nowhere the radio barks in our faces: 1085-Forthwith, 1085-Forthwith. Officers in pursuit need assistance. Repeat, officers in pursuit need assistance.

Al said it way before the message ended: "Go."

My adrenaline shot from zero to a hundred. It's like the job changes in an instant—one second, all is well, the next, burn like hell.

First priority: *Get there.* Lights, siren, roaring engine, the works. Because now it's real and you hear a cop yelling into his radio as he's chasing someone down and the perp is armed and then you hear all kinds of noises and hard breathing and you just don't know what's going on.

Get there.

Now maybe I was young and dumb, or maybe I just thought the S in Stanton I wore on my uniform chest stood for Superman. But as I drove, I was drooling to get my hands on this bad guy. I had everything—training, physical ability, drive. If I got my cuffs on the bad guy, that meant one less bad guy, sure, but it also meant I'd be a bigger, badder cop than I'd been before I got behind the wheel that night. The bad guy would be my trophy. I could bust the other guys' chops. "I got the guy. I beat you all."

Al and I rolled up to the scene and I slammed the brakes. I was out before the car had time to settle on its shocks. I spotted one of our guys chasing the suspect out on some train tracks below street level. I climbed over two fences (no, I didn't just smash through them, but I would've if I could've) and sprinted along a cement wall above the tracks.

They were about twenty-five yards ahead of me now. I knew I could catch them. But they headed for a tunnel and I needed to be down on the tracks to make it happen.

As soon as I jumped, I knew I was in trouble.

The top of the wall had been about six feet above the tracks. Had been. It was dark, so as I ran along the top of that wall, I couldn't see that the tracks sloped lower as they got closer to that tunnel. So there I am, airborne, expecting a no-sweat six-foot drop, and now I'm airborne a lot longer than I should be. The drop turned out to be more like twelve feet.

Crap.

My feet hit and I instinctively put my hands out to break my fall. Better prep time and a little more knowledge and maybe I'd have braced for the drop and rolled on landing. Hell, maybe I would've been so smooth I'd roll and pop to my feet, running without losing a step. Superman unleashed. None of that happened.

My feet and hands hit and I fell backward. It felt like forever, and maybe it was a full second, but I got up and spotted the guys running into the tunnel. Ha. Lucky sucker. I'm OK.

I went for my gun without looking, but couldn't get at it. Then I looked and it was weird. I couldn't get my fingers to curl around the grip. What the . . . ? Then I held up my hand and saw all the blood. My right palm had landed on something that severed tendons and nerves. I didn't know how bad it was at the time. All I knew was other cops were yelling, I was yelling, and blood was pouring down my arm into my sleeve and I'm so friggin' pissed because I'm out of the game.

Little did I know, but would find out after a year of surgeries and physical therapy on my hand, that I was out of the game permanently. I did everything I could. But back then, the NYPD required all officers to be able to handle the sixteen-pound force required to pull the double-action trigger on a standard-issue .38. My right hand couldn't hack it.

I learned the hard way that night about a lesson the Boy Scouts drill into every newbie: Good intentions matter, but if you impair yourself during a crisis, you're no good to the people around you and you become a liability for other first responders. Being overzealous is sometimes just as bad as doing too little when it comes to stopping those with malicious intent.

When one door closes, another opens, and this one came with a red velvet rope! That door was the entrance to the famous China Club, at the time the hottest nightclub in New York City, if not the world. Out of the public service, I turned to the private sector—specifically, club security, working as a bouncer for several of the city's best-known nightclubs. Luckily for me, club owners respected the ethics and professional skill set of an ex-NYPD officer. During my gigs as a bouncer, I was shot at, stabbed, punched, kicked, and pummeled. To be honest, I was probably in more danger than I was as a cop in the South Bronx.

While working at the nightclub Rascals, I met Jerry Glazebrook, a protection specialist. His credentials included serving as Secretary of State Henry Kissinger's chief of protective detail. Glazebrook explained what "executive protection" actually requires—skills I was sorely deficient in. Yes, I could stop a crime in action, save victims on the brink of death, and spot shady characters at a nightclub, but what about examining a space for security breaches? Making sure a vehicle was safe to drive? Enhancing security in a home or office? I realized that my skills as a former rookie cop paled in comparison to the experience of Jerry. He had operated as a security professional for the highest levels of U.S. government.

Thanks to Glazebrook's encouragement, I enrolled at the exclusive Executive Protection Institute (EPI)—my college and graduate school experience wrapped into one. If not for the patience and tutelage of Glazebrook, I'm certain I never would have gotten into this prestigious institution. At EPI, I learned what it takes to become a Secret Service–level protection specialist—situational awareness, strategic thinking, how to "read a room," protective formations, driving, and advance work. I was fortunate to learn close quarters combat and shooting skills from the legendary firearms instructor Pat Rogers, isshinryu karate from Master Tommy May, and evasive driving from Tony Scotti. And I wrangled an invitation to a course in detecting deception by the CIA's very best spy masters. Phil Houston literally wrote the book on how to detect deception (*Spy the Lie*). His ability to detect deception is fascinating, if not a little scary. Phil knows exactly when someone is lying and how to get the truth. Ultimately, the great instructors inspired me to pursue a Ph.D. of sorts in fighting crime from EPI.

Thanks to a combination of academic study and real-world application, I reached the cutting edge of personal security. For roughly a decade, I juggled EPI, the China Club, and an increasing number of personal executive protection assignments with various private investigation and executive protection agencies. I worked security for high-net-worth families in Aspen, Colorado, during the height of the holiday season. I protected royalty from Europe and the Middle East, as well as Americans such as [First Lady] Jacqueline Kennedy Onassis. I crossed paths with Police Commissioner Bill

Bratton, along with his left and right hands, John Miller and Jack Maple. Back then, the newly minted CompStat was just starting to put a dent in the city's crime rates. I partnered with Phil Houston, along with a few other former CIA officers, to form QVerity in November 2009. We would go on to investigate the tragic case of the missing infant Lisa Irwin (more on that in the first chapter).

A helpful dose of good luck and the word about town on the sheer diversity and strength of my different protection assignments eventually caught the attention of award-winning journalist Craig Horowitz, at that time a feature writer. In 2001, I was featured on the cover of *New York magazine,* with an eight-page profile.

However, the personal satisfaction of professional recognition in my hometown was short-lived. The tragic and world-changing 9/11 attacks made me realize that my prior efforts had done so little for most of the country. I decided to completely focus my new efforts on television, believing there was no better way to reach millions of ordinary, hardworking Americans. I was NBC News' first safety and security contributor for the *Today* show, ABC's first safety and security contributor for *Good Morning America*, and the focus of two *Dateline* specials.

I believe this manual is the natural next step. I hope it will reinforce the impact of my work on television. If reading *Prepared, Not Scared* teaches you more about safety and security, and you feel empowered yourself, then I've accomplished my goal.

CHAPTER ONE

Home Sweet Home Security

The Importance of Preventive Security

DO YOU PLAY THE LOTTERY? The likelihood that you will experience a property victimization of any kind—from having your car burglarized to a full-blown home invasion—*are far more likely than ever winning.*

Let's start with the cold, hard facts: There is a burglary in the United States every fifteen seconds. For one in four burglaries, at least one innocent person is inside the home. One in fifty American residences are burglarized each year and nearly one in ten of those turns violent. The chance that anyone in your family will be the victim of a home invasion? The chances are low, but we do know that every year, roughly 100 innocent Americans die in a home invasion. These chances rival those of deadly cancers, for which doctors and experts are constantly urging vigilance and screening—and something you might pay more attention to than home security. Why not start having the same attitude toward protecting your home? If your home is burglarized, the chance that someone will be home and the invasion turns violent is one in one thousand—the same chance any woman faces of dying of breast cancer in the next decade. And how often have you been advised to get a mammogram? Surely, your home safety needs to take a front seat as well.

Planning for the very worst—whether it be an attack on our country, an attack on your home, or an attack on your person—became such a focus of the U.S. government after 9/11 that the Homeland Security Department launched the Ready Initiative—a comprehensive database of practical, accessible information that could save your life. Ready.gov has guides and facts for Americans in every walk of life, and I can't recommend enough that you check out their site and put its advice into practice. https://www.ready .gov/make-a-plan puts fantastic information right at your fingertips, and the book you hold in your hands can help to amplify your future experiences. Like the Homeland Security Department, I want to prepare you for a worst-case scenario.

Education in safety and security is the best prevention from being hurt to begin with. I love and respect our nation's first responders. But I also understand that they are, literally, *responders*. By the time they are on the scene, tragedy and disaster have usually already struck. This is especially true of home invasions, as my first Stanton Story demonstrates anecdotally all too well.

Stanton Story: *Baby Lisa*

THE MOST HARROWING home invasion of my career involved every parent's worst nightmare: a kidnapped child. "Baby Lisa Irwin" made worldwide headlines back in 2011, and updates still surface in places like People.com and other outlets to this day. The case captivated everyone and it could be boiled down to a simple home invasion, an easy crime of opportunity after a loser found, and followed through on, an easy entry.

That's how it happens, folks. On the day you least expect it, the day you let your guard down, the bad stuff happens. Jeremy and Deborah Irwin prioritized home security, just like most people, but a lowlife cashed in on the one day they were careless. What happened to them could happen to anybody.

In October 4, 2011, the Irwins lived in a small, one-story house in Kansas City, Missouri. That morning, they realized their ten-month-old daughter Lisa was missing. They called the police and their lives have never been the same.

Soon after the kidnapping, I flew down to KC with the QVerity team and interrogated the Irwins for hours. I told them that my client was Baby Lisa—and if they were guilty, there would be hell to pay. To their credit, they opened up to the QVerity team and we were able to piece together the night's events. We used CIA-honed skills to detect any deception on their parts. We identified exactly zero attempts to lie to us.

Their story: On October 4, Deborah Irwin was an overworked mom who just wanted to unwind. Jeremy was still at work, so she had a few drinks that evening and indulged their three children by letting them sleep in the main bedroom with her.

Jeremy returned late that night to find Deborah asleep with kids, the lights on, and the front door unlocked. When he saw the kids in their bed, he argued with Deborah, but she was still groggy and in no condition to talk things out. Despite the argument, as they told it later to the QVerity team, the Irwins thought they were in a good place. Jeremy cooled off and turned in. After all, why be mad at your wife for loving your kids so much that she needed them close to her?

At around 4:00 a.m., Deborah was half-awake and sobering up. At first, she thought she was dreaming. But a voice in her head urged her awake. Something was wrong; she just didn't know what. Once they realized that Baby Lisa was missing and the window in her room ajar, they called Kansas City police and the nightmare began.

It wasn't just the news coverage. The Irwins were painted as suspects and, eventually, murderers, even though no evidence connected them to Baby Lisa's disappearance and no trace of Baby Lisa—alive or dead—had ever been found. Evidence and witness accounts pointed to an unsophisticated low-life trying to score—an unidentified man was spotted in the neighborhood before dawn carrying a baby—but no other leads have surfaced.

Five years later, the Baby Lisa disappearance remains an open case. I believe she's out there, still alive, sent to her fate by some addict who sold her for drug money. But I also use her case as the ultimate cautionary tale for parents and home owners. Understand what home security really means and what it takes to achieve it. Because you just never know what could happen.

HOME SECURITY QUESTIONS

THIS CHAPTER WILL OUTLINE exactly how to protect those things, effectively, and without fear. Don't hesitate to take that extra time out of your life to better secure the lives of those you love. Investing in your security is investing in your safety—and perhaps even your survival.

Our homes—big or small, rich or poor—are our Sanctuaries, our Havens, our Castles. For most Americans, our home is the most valuable asset we'll ever own. That's an understatement for those who are parents—for parents, and for so many of us, the home protects our most valuable assets: children, self, and loved ones.

Let's arm you with an expert-tested list of key questions that helps you brainstorm about the worst mistakes people can make. Although I'll cover later how to take realistic steps for notifying the police and getting help, the best way to stop home invasions is before they start. This list of questions will help you to identify red flags and effectively remove potentially dangerous habits you may have fallen into unknowingly.

Have you taken advantage of the free (and invaluable) services from your local police department?	Start from the outside corners of your property and work your way in (in the security field, this is called "concentric circle protection"). Security should intensify as we move closer to your family. Call your local police department, and learn the crime statistics in your area. If, for example, cars are broken into, do you need to be focused more on your vehicle than on your house? You can also make an appointment, for free, with your local police, and they will gladly come to your home and advise you on your property's most vulnerable spots.
Is your home well lit?	On a dark night, watch your home for a few minutes from the street. Can you see where people are moving or sitting in the home? Are all entrances and the walkway to your home well lit, meaning that burglars will be deterred from the property, in fear of being seen or recognized?
Does your home offer tantalizing views of its interior?	Have you mitigated this with blinds, shades, and securing and hiding valuables from outside view?
Do you have a good sense of how your home could be physically breached?	Can the second story of your home be accessed? Do you have two locks on all exterior doors and at least one lock on every window?
Have you considered installing motion lights or a camera system?	If yes, use their advertising and signage widely across the front and back of your property to prevent a criminal from casing your property.
Does every door leading into and out of the home have a lock that you've invested in?	That means at least two locks, including a slap lock for every exterior door.
When you exit your home, do you always lock the door behind you?	

Are you testing your security investments every few weeks?	Security systems, motion lights, and cameras are only as good as your engaging them.
Have you changed the factory settings of your garage door opener and your home security system, and do you change their passwords often?	
Does everyone with access to your home security system have their own code?	Did you know that your cleaner, your dog sitter, and your architect can all use separate key codes to enter your home? That way, if a breach or burglary takes place, police will know who was home at the time.
Bad Guy POV: Are you an advertisement for thieves?	In today's world of social media, people are walking billboards. We put out to the world who we are—we've become our own PR advertising company. What you don't realize is that you're advertising to thieves. I would venture to say that in today's world of Facebook, Instagram, and Twitter, the percentage of friends and family is far less than acquaintances. My advice? Do a self-review and audit of your social media. You'd be in awe of what you are telling potential bad guys: geo-time-stamped photos? Photos of you on vacation (so people know you're not home)? Bad guys no longer need to "case" a home; they only need to be "linked in" (pun intended). When you're preyed upon—and you ask now, "Who would do this to me?"—you've made your list that much bigger by using social media irresponsibly.
Are you aware and on the lookout for "inside jobs"?	We've all been guilty of it, including myself—whether it's dry cleaning, pizza, or a package being delivered—we've all let complete strangers into our home. They are getting an up close and personal view of who's in your house. They can also take note of whether you have a dog or an alarm system, and your different entrance points—assessing your overall vulnerability. You'd be amazed at how many thefts across America are actually "inside jobs."

How well do you vet your vendors?	Speaking of "inside jobs," your nanny, babysitters, pool guy, plumber, and roofers all need to be vetted, because all will gain intimate knowledge of your home, your family, and even your trash!
	If these vendors have honorable intentions, they will not be put off by your questions. In fact, these providers will welcome your pseudo-interviews as a good sign: Their client is smart and on top of things, meaning they're likely to pay their bills.
	RULE OF THREES: 3 Questions ➜ Do you have three people within three miles of me that can recommend you? ➜ Did you have at least three different jobs within the last three weeks? ➜ What are your top three priorities when taking on a job? (Safety should be one of them.)

KNOW YOUR BURGLAR TYPES

Professional Thief

Does this for a living, all while holding down a legitimate job so people don't ask questions. This soft-spot expert knows which doors, windows, cars, and locks are easiest to breach. It's hard to stop a criminal with this much experience, but motion-activated lights, breach-proof doors, dead bolts, and closed and locked windows with drawn shades are great ways to start.

Opportunistic Thief

You know them, but you don't. It's the son of your yard worker, who could gain entry by stealing a key from his dad. It's the niece of the manicurist, who you tell you'll be away for the weekend. These aren't necessarily evil people, but they're either hurting or greedy, and if they see an opening, they'll take it. Remember that your small talk can be a big opportunity for a person with bad intentions.

Addiction Thief

In the clutches of a disease, these victims of addiction will put aside all logic and compassion to score either your money or your prescription drugs. Don't tell people what medicines you use, and be sure to keep any cash in your home fully out of sight.

SEASON, TIME, AND DURATION

Warm weather helps the bad guys: Burglaries increase across the country in July and August, and are most prevalent year-round in the South.

Most homes are burglarized between 10:00 a.m. and 3:00 p.m.—when they likely aren't occupied. Remember, a criminal is hoping not to run into you: no witnesses to their crime, and no roadblocks to their score. In this chapter, you'll find security guidelines especially tailored to those crucial hours.

The low-life who enters your home is usually there for ten whole minutes. Why? If you do have an alarm that goes off, they need to get away, but police usually take more than that time to arrive. Most invaders are not searching for a fight. Any altercation slows down the culprit and makes it more likely the police will arrive in time for an arrest. When a home invasion turns violent, 70 percent of the time, the family and the criminals already knew each other and burglary was not the main reason for the home invasion. (We'll cover other types of home invasions in Chapter 10.)

Can where you live tell you whether you'll be burglarized?

CAUTION! Do not listen to cheesy lists that tell you "Top 10 Cities for Burglaries" or "Worst States for Break-Ins"! Why? As the FBI writes at the top of its annual crime report, "Figures used in this report were submitted voluntarily by law enforcement agencies throughout the country. Individuals using these tabulations are cautioned against drawing conclusions by making direct comparisons between cities." That's right—cities have the right to withhold their information. So all you can learn from digging into these crime rates is which are the most insecure places of those that submitted data to the feds! And to take it a step further—what if ten families didn't report a burglary to the police? Rankings get cloudy pretty quickly.

All that being said, I think we're well within our rights to talk about national trends as the FBI describes them. So what's going up, and what's going down?

- *Robbery is on the decline (down 2 percent).*

- *Burglary is on the decline (down 6 percent).*

- *Larceny and theft rates are lowering (down 3 percent).*

- *Motor vehicle theft rose in 2017 more than any other crime (up by more than 4 percent). The chapter on car safety will address this.*

HIGH-RISK ENTRY POINTS

LET'S TALK ABOUT the weakest entry points and what to do about improving your home security.

Windows

Not only are windows weaker than walls, they're necessarily see-through, which means criminals are able to use windows to degrade your security. Habits, object placement, and home lighting are all visible through windows.

Every window in your home should have a lock option and a shade or curtain—no exceptions.

Walk around the outside of your home once or twice with the mind of home invader. Which windows look easy to break or climb through? Through which windows can someone from the outside see the most expensive items, which could tempt them to open a window from the outside or break a window. After your homework, make sure each of these windows has locks, and curtains or blinds that can be drawn at strategic moments—like when most of the family is gone.

For a list of the best window brands, and window locks, with security in mind, there's more for you in the "Let's Get Physical" section of this chapter.

Drapes, drapes, drapes. Bay windows are a great view for you—and the bad guys. Close your blinds when you sleep or when you leave your home.

Big beautiful bay windows—like you look in with awe at Saks Fifth Avenue—potential intruders are looking at your possessions. This is where the security offered by drapes and blinds can make a huge difference when you're not at home.

Garage Doors

A garage is one of the most vulnerable parts of the home—mainly because people don't hang out in the garage and, in fact, usually avoid it.

You would not believe how many people close their garage door and believe that their home is secure. The physical weakness and technological weakness (the ability to hack a code or an industry button opener) of a standard garage door cannot be stressed enough.

An attached garage offers a double whammy for bad guys. It's usually easy to get into the garage, and then equally uncomplicated to open the door leading to the home's interior. Remember to change your garage door code every few weeks, and take the locks to your garage-to-house interior door just as seriously as you take them on your front door. ALWAYS lock the door between your home and your garage—and make sure it's a strong, solid, preferably metal door.

Bad guys love to pry open a garage door, or even open it (easily) using a factory-setting opener button they bought online. If they then see a flimsy or open door leading to the home's interior, they're as good as inside.

Garage bandits

We've covered securing the door that connects your home to your garage, but don't forget that similar structures on any property are also highly vulnerable to theft—sheds, barns, and pool houses included. Make sure any security measures you install in your home extend to every structure on your property. Even if people aren't living inside them, a secure shed, for example, that successfully rebuffs a perpetrator will signal that the home on the property is just as secure. I recommend door security bars, locks for shed and pool house windows, and ensuring that your home alarm system features triggers in these outposts—as well as alarm stickers and signs.

Remember, any measure that turns a criminal away from your property could save your life.

Sliding Doors at the Back of the House

If you have an alarm system, make sure to put decals and signs at the BACK of your home as well as the front! Criminals case the back of a home first, because it's typically less visible from the street—so neighbors are less likely to call police.

Yes, we know they're beautiful—but sliding doors further deteriorate your home's rear exterior by presenting a relatively large area of weakness. So what can you do to secure them?

- ► Curtains, blinds, drapes—when you're not home, make sure no one can see into your home.
- ► Invest in a door security bar for every set of sliding door in your home. Security bars ensure that no door can ever be opened or jimmied if it's locked—and that a perpetrator would need to break a space in the door the size of his body to get inside. In an attack scenario, that's buying you time to make the next move. These are about $20 at Walmart—no excuses!

Second Floor

A home invader adept at climbing into a home is known in the protection business as a second-story man—they're that common. When locking your home for a vacation, always remember to lock your second- and third-floor windows.

Be wary of where you leave your ladder. Second-story men will use your ladder to gain entry into your home. Why? Families tend to leave entries unlocked on the second floor—balconies, porch doors, windows—you name it.

Circle your second or third floor and determine what openings can currently be locked—and lock them. Make a note of which openings need locks, and commit to purchasing them as soon as possible (your windows are most likely your main culprit).

Next-level tip: breach- and bullet-resistant doors

Can't afford a safe room? With construction technology advancing as fast as it is, safe rooms are quickly becoming a thing of the past for very wealthy or very security-conscious households. Enter the breach-proof door—a door that looks like anything you'd like out of an interior decorating magazine, but weighs five hundred pounds when locked and is impossible to open, because steel bars pass through the entire door and into the surrounding walls. These doors exist at every price point, and for roughly the cost of a weekend vacation, these top-of-the-line protectors could be yours.

Whether at home or at work, investing in a state-of-the art door is a smart, middle-ground solution between owning a firearm and doing nothing at all. What puts these doors in the "Goldilocks" zone for me is that they afford discreet protection. They no longer look like bank-vault doors out of a comic book movie, like they did a few years ago. Breach-resistant, bullet-resistant, and security doors offer peace of mind in an emergency . . . and once they're installed, you don't have to do a thing.

Without further ado, here are my recommendations for the best door investments out there:

Total Security Solutions
Theses doors come in several commercial varieties, offering different levels of security and materials. They range from polymers to reinforced steal.
www.tssbulletproof.com

SwissShade Security
This company's main offering actually focuses on windows, mainly bullet-resistant ones. Now, they offer bullet-resistant doors, in a wide range of styles that can blend into any style.
www.swissshade.com

Secret Door by Hidden Passageway
I'm personally a fan of this type of door, and I've incorporated something like this into my own home.
www.hiddenpassageway.com

Armor Concepts
First off, this company immediately tells you that they don't sell doors. What they do is reinforce your current door and door frame. If your entry-point doors are heavy and strong and you feel comfortable with not having additional protections like bullet resistance, this option will be your most wallet-friendly.
www.armorconcepts.com

Door Devil
Similar to Armor Concepts, DD's unique approach is reinforcing what you already own.
www.doordevil.com

MODERATE-RISK ENTRY POINTS
Front Doors and Windows:
Security First, Then Fashion

Conceding that we live in a world that's largely focused on form over function (as well as keeping up with the Joneses), I realized that no one wants what looks like a bank vault as the front door.

The last few years have yielded major construction advancement in polymers and light metals. Metal or hard plastic breach-proof doors now look exactly like wood, as well as any other material that's fashionable for entryways.

The same is true of windows and locks. Breach-proof materials once looked like something out of a science-fiction movie—now, they look like something out of *Architectural Digest*. I recommend using *Consumer Reports* for any security purchase. While choosing security first, fashion second is always the right choice, review and rating digests will feature real-world feedback at every price point. No matter your budget, secure home exterior options are there for you, and must be taken into account as you create a secure household.

For every door that bars your home from the outside, install a heavy-duty dead-bolt clock with at least a one-inch throw bolt (the longer, the stronger). This measure should be your bare minimum—I recommend going further by also installing a slap lock to each of these doors. You'll find that every hotel room in America features one of these—and for good reason. Unless a perpetrator can kick a door down, a slap-locked door is staying closed.

Chain locks are not helpful for keeping a door closed, and should only be used when a trusted visitor is handing you an item. Think UPS, FedEx, or a bill from the utility company. If you haven't seen the provider before, but are assured that the representative is trustworthy, use the chain lock. And of course, if the package is too large for the space allowed by the chain, ask the representative to come back at another time if you feel any measure of hesitation.

But mostly, I'd say: Don't install one and then be tempted to use it. If you want to see someone before you open a solid door, install a peephole. If you feel any hesitation in fully opening a door, I err toward not opening it with a chain lock attached, either.

STANTON STORY: *Home Invasion*

THIS STORY COMES TO ME from a well-known and beloved retired NYPD police chief whose daughter was well-educated (in academics and street smarts) by her father. She was studying alone in her room one night when she looked up and saw a large male intruder in her doorway. He said, "I'm gonna close the door, and if you leave, I'll kill everyone in this house." He then exited, closing the door. She made sure the door couldn't be opened again by squeezing a chair under the doorknob, and then jumped out the window, ran to a neighbor's house, and called the police, saving every member of her family in the process.

WORST-CASE SCENARIO:
YOU'RE HOME, AND SO ARE THE BAD GUYS

LET'S SAY YOU'RE HOME and trouble comes snooping around. The same way all our grandmothers told us about going out to play in the wintertime is the same counsel I'll give everyone on home security: layering. I can't tell you the number of people who feel safe and secure in their home because of "I have a dog," "I have a security system," "I have a firearm." Well, unless it's all of the above, you're not layering. As I've proven on many a segment on NBC and ABC, your so-called security dog is anything but.

Let's review a few of the key steps or "layers" you can put in place to improve the odds in your favor should this less likely but more concerning scenario play out:

In the Dark of the Night, Let There Be Light

Motion-activated lights are easier than ever to purchase and install, and security-enhancing guards for front doors, walkways, side doors, and, especially, the back of your home. Nothing scares a potential intruder like an unexpected beam of light tracking his every move.

But remember, these lights don't secure anything if they're not working. Test your own motion-activated lights at regular intervals, choosing a different day of the week to walk around your home at night—I recommend monthly tests.

Your alarm system is only as good as how frequently you activate it. I can't tell you how many break-ins . . .

Who Let the Dogs Out?

Your dog, no matter what size, is one layer of security whenever it barks.

But don't count on your canine as your first or sole security measure.

While a dog is in fact a deterrent, you don't want to put that family member in unnecessary danger. Better to employ the "all of the above" approach via investing in a strong security system. There are many economical ways to approach this, including investing in good locks, motion lights, etc.

Don't be lazy when you do hear your dog barking—the dog is following its natural instincts, and could be saving your life by alerting you to something out of the ordinary.

When your dog does bark, get up and check it out. This is both a safe and a logical response on your part as well as reinforcing to the dog that you react to its alerts. And never punish your dog for barking at strangers—you don't want to inadvertently train your dog not to warn you.

Properly Answer Your Door

When someone knocks on your door, get in the habit of not opening it. Opening the door accomplishes most of the work for the bad guy.

I like to say that properly answering your door means not answering your door. There are two approaches to answering a secure door: low-tech and high-tech.

1. Low-Tech

The low-tech can be just as effective as the high-tech route, and these simple steps are key to warding off a home invasion. Use your windows, a peephole, or any point of observation to see who's actually at the door.

Better to be rude than wrong—keep the door closed, and ask loudly, through it, who's there. This important step in throwing off a perpetrator signals that at least one person is home—even if the visitor is attempting to deceive you.

2. High-Tech

The high-tech route is already standard in many apartment buildings—an intercom, or even a camera that can transmit information on who's at the door directly to you. Today, there are even smartphone apps that can monitor your home and show you who's at the door when you're on vacation—I recommend investing in these apps; they often pay off.

For the even more technically inclined, invisible pressure pads for your driveway and walkways leading to your house notify you before a visitor gets within reach of your door.

With today's ever advancing camera and microprocessing abilities, and their lower and lower prices as technology improves, why not take advantage of these new tools?

These questions can help determine if it's worth it to you to open the door:

- If they answer that they're from a delivery or utilities company: Can I see your ID?

    Be sure to actually take a few seconds to scan their identification. Many criminals, seeking to enter a space, will simply hold up an official-looking card or piece of paper.

    Check for the logo of the delivery company.

    If anything about their identification looks off, ask the visitor, "Can you come back later? I'm really busy right now." Saying something like "That doesn't look right!" or "Where's the UPS logo?" could raise tension and, therefore, the visitor's aggression level. Many criminals seek to punish those who have "found them out."

If any ID looks suspicious, be sure to call their "company" to alert them of fraud—or just plain bad policy and badges. "Oh, that was a 1-800-Teddy-Bear deliveryman? Could you improve your identification process? I truly had no idea who was at my door."

▶ If the visitor says they're from a smaller, local company that may not issue badges to employees, ask for a number to their main office—then ask if "John Smith" is out on delivery right now, in your neighborhood specifically.

▶ If the visitor is meant to be there, they won't flinch at your reasonable precautions. If they get mad or visibly annoyed—that's a red flag. Consider calling the police at any sign of aggression, as well as simply asking them to return at a different time.

▶ Answering a door should always be done at YOUR level of comfort, with circumstances in mind. For example—your husband is home, watching the game with his buddies? Answering the door is likely fine. But home alone, late at night? Maybe not so much.

If you do decide to open the door, get in the habit of conversing and collecting any packages *outside* your door—don't let anyone you haven't vetted inside. Welcoming a visitor inside means showcasing everything a criminal could potentially take. Don't tempt a crime of opportunity from someone down on their luck.

▶ If someone on the other side of the door has malicious intentions, severely degraded security gains a foothold in your home if you open it. So while we all like to be courteous, kind, and neighborly, err on the side of caution. "Good guys" won't mind that in the least.

Locks and doors

An investment lock is only as good as the door it's inside.

Home security needs to be a mindset. Most homes are not built with an acceptable level of home security. By acceptable, we mean that most houses don't have the inherent ability to meet the threats posed by those who would otherwise do us harm. If you don't understand that some people do want to do you harm, you're not motivated enough to make changes.

You don't need to turn your home into a fortress. You need to identify weak spots, address them, and keep a vigilant mindset.

Remember that most standard-installation locks are insufficient to prevent a break-in. Your first step should be enhancing the lock hardware of your home. Additional dead bolts can do a world of good. I prefer triple-locking a door: a dead bolt at the top, a dead bolt at the bottom, and a dead bolt in the traditional center spot of the door.

Security is measured by: "How long does it take the bad guy to overcome my safeguards?" Anyone with the right equipment can get into a house, unfortunately. Your safety measures need to buy you enough time to call the authorities, leave the home, or defend yourself.

The following circumstances are going to be tough to speak to, because there are so many different scenarios—but if you take the following as a template, common sense will dictate how to prepare for an array of security-breach experiences. If you have to think for more than three seconds, you've exponentially put you and your family in greater danger already. Be prepared, not scared with the following steps for several different scenarios:

Scenario...

Your husband took the primary car away on a fishing trip, so there are no cars in the driveway. You're in your bedroom watching TV. You turned the TV off, and you're drifting off to sleep. Your children, aged seven and ten, are in bed asleep, in their separate bedrooms. It's a little past midnight. You hear breaking glass and multiple footsteps upstairs. You now realize your home has been invaded.

The empty driveway and dark house tipped off the intruder, falsely, that no one was home.

Action

- Call 9-1-1 as soon as possible. Even if you can't speak, keep them on the line so they know your exact location.

- Next, if you have a cellphone with you, use texting to inform as many geographically close friends and family what's happening. Ask them to call 9-1-1 and tell them to describe your home and your children to police.

- Make a decision based on intuition and any signals from the intruder on how you'll approach other family members in the home. When it comes to your children, go with your gut—do you leave them sleeping, hoping the intruder takes your valuables and leaves? Or do you run to their rooms and attempt to leave through a window? The choice is yours, and there is no case study that can tell you what to do.

- Attempt to exit the home, however you can and as quickly as you can. Run to a neighbor's home and ask them for help.

- If you can't leave the house, then find a weapon.

Scenario...

Same scenario, but you've fallen asleep in the basement. Now, the intruder is on the first floor—in between you and your children. While my advice would be anathema to any mother, here's how I believe you save your children:

Action

- Go through a door, a window, or running up the stairs and out the front door. Do not risk crossing paths with an intruder to get to your children—you will be attacked, and you will be little help to your children if you are injured and the intruder learns that children are in the home. Statistically, the intruder will leave within ten minutes—your family's chance of survival increases if he gets in and gets out.

▶ Go to a neighbor's house or use your cellphone to call 9-1-1 as quickly as possible.

▶ This is just one of countless scenarios—and the point of this exercise is to show you that sometimes, action that increases your family's secur ity are counterintuitive to your more natural, basic instincts.

▶ In times of stress and emergency, it's research shows that survival results from a default to strategic thinking, rather than thinking emotionally.

Scenario...

You've just dropped the kids off at school, and now you're back at the house. Doing laundry on the second floor, you hear a window breaking on the first floor. You're covering for your wife today, so intruders must have been casing the house—she's usually grocery shopping on Tuesdays, and there's no car in the driveway on this day every week—but they entered from the back of the house and couldn't see your parked minivan, clearly indicating that someone was home.

You are a man alone (thank goodness the kids are at school). You have a physical disability, so you're not as mobile as the typical middle-aged man. You make the educated guess (from the sheer force hinted at with the sounds of shattered glass) that the intruders are physically stronger than you are. You own a firearm, and it's easily reachable. Your cellphone, on the other hand, is still on the counter in the kitchen—on the first floor.

Action

▶ Based on this scenario, I would most definitely get to my weapon as stealthily and quickly as possible.

▶ Once accomplished, I would secure in place, then yell out to the intruders, letting them know that I'm armed and calling the police.

▶ At this point, depending upon the intruders, I'd either wait for them to leave or fire a round into a piece of heavy furniture, so the shot would effectively let them know I'm truly armed and mean business.

Scenario...

You're just taking the keys out of your backpack after a grueling basketball practice to find that you don't need to unlock your back door—it's already open, the keyhole surrounded by knife marks —the knife that must have been used to jimmy it open. Inside, you can see your father's cookbooks strewn across the kitchen floor.

Like anyone would be, at fifteen years old, you're paralyzed with fear, standing like a statue on your welcome mat, still just outside the house. You're dehydrated, tired, and mentally drained from practice. Your home is small but secure—why didn't your alarm system go off? You suddenly remember last year, when your parents had to cut back on date nights to pay for it. No one in your family is home—that's why you have a key for after practice on Thursdays.

Action

▶ You could run as fast as you can to the neighbors' house, tell them what's going on, and contact the police.

▶ Or, get to a safe distance (meaning you could not be seen or heard by the intruders, and you are also off your property), and call 9-1-1.

Scenario...

You're cleaning your shower with the music pumping and feeling great—you called in sick to work to finally get around to that spring cleaning. A few songs and a lot of bleach in, you hear the lock to the door click shut, and the young man who's been cutting your lawn for the last few months is suddenly within two feet of you, asking for your debit card's PIN.

You're a woman, and while you're a few years older than the per-petrator, he definitely happens to be stronger. You and your hus-band bought a firearm for this very nightmare, but of course, you haven't locked and loaded for your spring cleaning session. Your gun? Under your bed, sixty feet away. Your debit card is in your back pocket—you usually have it in your wallet, but for some reason at the store that day, you slipped it into your jeans as you hustled to get to yoga. You've pictured these scenarios before, and always planned to offer up all your money if something like this happened. But the thought of taking this guy to an ATM—which means driving with him—makes your skin crawl.

Action

- Here the cards are really stacked against you. Mental chess is para-mount—you must judge the temperament and potentiality of what is happening versus what this could escalate into. Rape? Homicide? Or is it just the debit card and PIN?

- What you believe to be imminent will dictate your actions and reactions.

- If it's just the cash, hand over the card and PIN.

- If it's rape, that's a judgment call as there are various ways to fight back, both mentally and physically—which we'll cover using my experience in the field and expert opinions in chapter 3 about personal safety.

- Finally, if you feel that your life is in danger, about to end, and that there are no other options available to you, you use your critical think-ing skills to get to that weapon.

Scenario...

Curling up next to your wife in bed, you couldn't imagine a more beautiful summer night. The kids are asleep, and you're dozing off. You wanted to stay up a little later to get some work done, but after a glass of wine with a big pasta dinner on a Saturday night, and a movie with the kids, you know you're done for the night. Suddenly, you feel the barrel of a gun against your temple. A voice tells you, "Your children are locked in their rooms, and your dog is dead. Your wife will be too if you don't drive us to your office, right now."

You don't have a lot of money, but you do have a great job with access to all of your law firm's computers' passwords—and right now, your company is representing plaintiffs in a class action lawsuit. The first place your mind goes? Whoever has a gun to your head is working for the corporation that your team is up against. Picturing your children in danger sends your whole body into fight-or-flight mode—you're sweating, your face gets hot, and your only thought is that at the end of this, they're OK—even if you're dead. Hearing that your dog is dead only further disorients you—and as your heart beats out of your chest, you hope your children didn't see him die. After a night up late, you usually don't set your home security system—after all, what are the odds that someone would rob you in the hours between 2:00 a.m. and 6:00 a.m.—when the kids wake up.

Action

- ▶ This scenario is the hardest for me to even think about. A good human being has been put in an impossible situation by a bad human being—there are no right answers.

- ▶ But right now, your attacker holds the power, and fighting back with a gun to your head could quickly escalate into you losing your life. My gut reaction says . . . unless you are John Wick or Bill Stanton (i.e., a trained defense professional, or a service member), you comply. But again, there is not a silver bullet here.

EXPERT INTERVIEW
Dan O'Connor

I WORKED FOR THE CIA for twenty-six years and retired twelve years ago. When I left "the Agency," as we call it, I opened up my own private security firm, The O'Connor Group. There are certain things I can't talk about, but what I can talk about is what you'll read here. A large part of my time at the Agency (meaning many, many years there) was spent protecting "the directors." By that I mean directors of Central Intelligence, or the highest up of the highest up in our national intelligence agencies. I was a supervisor and manager for the teams that traveled with these Directors, whether it be down the street or to foreign countries to totally ensure that the destinations were as secure as humanly possible. Eventually, my passion for protection led me to fight for legislation allowing us to protect the families of these directors—because no man, or woman, is an island. With the five directors and their direct reports under my care, it's safe to say I learned the most effective safety and security practices of the modern era.

Today, I apply my experience to my business in executive protection, which I've owned and operated for over a decade. At first I thought I'd consult on security issues after my government service, but a trustworthy friend offered me some jarring perspective that ultimately moved my goal post: I had served five directors (fairly unique to the Agency), had traveled internationally with them more times than I could count, and had arranged that every single one of those trips be safe, secure, and successful for hundreds of people, often in a dangerous host country. When I was weighing my next move, this friend asked me, "How do Fortune 500 companies travel? Do you think they'd travel with you, fifteen to twenty in a group? If I'm a CEO, do I want someone behind the scenes who knows what he's doing if I have to travel to a country in political turmoil to seal a deal?" I knew where he was going with this. He said, "From a consulting perspective, once you tell anyone sitting across from you at the table your résumé, they will want you to do the security, not the person or company you're recommending." It's true. I had shed the blood, sweat, and tears behind the success of Senior Intelligence Service—SIS—for more than half of my career.

My friend was right—once executives at risk of danger or under threat heard my story, they wanted me to devise their security apparatus.

Daniel O'Connor is the founder of The O'Connor Group, a company that offers international security solutions. Dan's career has crossed decades, continents, countries, and cultures. He worked for the CIA from 1979 to 2005, serving as the chief of personal security for the last five CIA directors and their deputies. He has also served as the CIA's chief administrator of U.S. facilities in Europe, as well as Central and South America.

With Children

I F YOU'RE OPEN TO IT, get your children's fingerprints recorded by your local police department. Why? From petty crimes committed by minors (graffiti comes to mind—and you swear your teen is innocent!), to the nightmare of your child missing and then, for example, law enforcement finds a child either alive or deceased, your child's identity will be ruled in or ruled out with certainty very quickly. The fingerprinting process also acquaints children with their local police station, with interacting with police, and with seeing that their parents trust police—all sentiments and memories that could come in handy later on if your child is in trouble.

In the same vein, be sure to keep current, realistic photos of your child—very easy to do in the age of smartphones.

Once your children are at the age where they leave your sight (think preschool), it's important to talk with them about the all-important "code word" concept. You don't need to tell your child, "Here's what you do if you're kidnapped and you can get ahold of us"—just introduce them to this safety trick by telling them it can be used whenever a grown-up is making them scared or uncomfortable. Pick a phrase with your children that wouldn't stand out as a "help word" of sorts to perpetrators—for example, no "banana" and no "Bring me a chocolate bar."

This simple exercise is a great example of teaching kids about safety and security in a way that doesn't scare them, but can also produce incredible results in avoiding irrevocable danger. In other words—a lot of bang for very little buck. Remember to close the conversation with, "When you say this, I'll come get you right away." Mental security is essential in helping children to make the right decision when danger strikes. If you're scaring your child, they don't absorb the helpful information, and that means your well-intentioned conversation's only effect was fright. Tailor what you're saying to your audience.

I especially think sentences like, "How is Aunt Jen doing?" or, "How was work today?" If your child is ever in that terrible situation, he or she will know they've filled you in on their situation without adding more danger. And it doesn't just have to be some heinous kidnapping situation—it can be any uncomfortable situation, like being taken to a playdate that's rubbing them the wrong way.

On a lighter note, this "trick" is also great for teens in an uncomfortable situation—a party that's spiraled out of control, a team dinner where they drank too much, or even for tweens, a sleepover where they're desperately homesick. Your shared "code sentence" means the child will get picked up quickly and discreetly . . . and that you, the parent, need to make up the reason. "I just remember we have a family dinner tomorrow with our relative from out-of-town . . . I need Suzy well-rested!" No social suicide here!

For Children: Explaining What to Do in a Shooting

Teach children to get behind something hard, and to stay there without moving, as quickly as possible. Phrases to use that aren't too jarring go something like—*What would you do if someone came into your classroom and tried to shoot someone?* Repeat that they should lie on the floor or move along the floor to get behind something hard. Why can't they move? *The police are coming in the room to stop the bad guy, and if you stay on the floor, they know you're a good guy. If you stand, the police could make a mistake.*

All of this is deeply upsetting, and may seem extreme. But from what we've seen in the news lately, tragedies seem to surround us. Consider this type of frank conversation with your children if you think they would find it helpful, and be able to use what you tell them.

For any age, in my experience it is more effective to run than to get on the ground. Tragically, what we're seeing in shootings carried out by evil madmen today is that the victims are often trapped, whether it be in a movie theater or a church. If you are trapped, get behind hard objects by staying low as quickly as you can. When is your best opportunity to run? When the perpetrator is reloading.

Residence

Much like the codeword concept, designate a room or space in your home as a meeting place if something feels wrong. I like to call this "the safe haven." If Mom or Dad is arguing with someone, if you're home alone and you hear strange noises, go to the safe haven and Mom or Dad will come get you when the issue is resolved. This concept is effective training for, sadly, the seemingly rampant frequency of shootings in public spaces—from churches to grade schools. The idea of looking for, finding, and remembering secure spaces will serve your child well, should he or she ever need shelter in the heat of the moment.

Whether you love or hate the NRA, one way to avoid robbery, burglary, or a home invasion is to place an NRA sticker next to your alarm sticker (or on its own, if you don't have an alarm system). You can get these for free at any NRA outpost. I've found this to be especially effective in urban areas. When a potential criminal sees that sign, whether you have a gun or not, whether you support the Second Amendment or not, that perpetrator thinks one of two things: "I'll try somewhere else," or, "I'm still going in, but I better leave the minute I hear something." Plus, if they're casing the twenty or so residences on your street, they'll stop to read that sticker and to contemplate what I've just laid out—so that means that even using the sticker buys you time. See someone suspicious checking out your NRA sticker? Call the police, and report that someone's been loitering around your home's entrance.

It goes without saying that if you have an alarm, you should have their sticker and signs around your property. Even if you don't have an alarm, most security companies sell stickers and posters online. Another indicator I recommend, even if it's not the whole truth: Many hardware stores sell a sign that reads, "This property is under 24-hour surveillance." Is your home decked out with cameras? Probably not—but any tactic that deters and dismays a criminal is worth employing.

If this falls within your home budget, I recommend replacing your home's exterior doors and your home's bedroom doors with "reinforced doors." These can be found at most hardware stores, and there are less expensive options for reinforcing doors you already have.

For residences of any income, I recommend leaving lights on when you leave the home. As Bill Stanton has repeatedly said: Most thieves looking to score do not want to run into people. Unlike in the great film *Home Alone*, criminals are likely to move on if they think someone is home.

Alarm Systems

If you can afford an alarm system (and not just the sticker!), I recommend you buy one and use it consistently. You never need an alarm system until you need an alarm system, and you do not want to spend the time, money, and emotional energy to install one after a tragedy or a simple robbery.

My next suggestion: Get the version that offers a single panic button or several panic buttons around your home. These immediately notify the security company and law enforcement, and when you're terrified or weakened, it helps to know that all you need to do is press one button. Alarm systems are often required for home insurance, but note the fine print of your coverage: Do you need an alarm system simply to be installed, or to be used daily? Pay close attention to the terms.

The best thing about using an alarm system is counterintuitive—walking into your home, whether it be after a long day at work or a long time away, and knowing that *no one is here, and no one was here*. An alarm system is only as good as your using it. That said, I've also seen that simple stickers alone can be remarkably effective.

Code Words and "Callbacks" and Rings

Let's say you truly have a "false alarm"—your toddler pushes the panic button, you thought you had a home intruder on your hands but it was actually your cat, or quite simply, the system malfunctions. Once you manage to turn the alarm off, you will get a call from the company asking for your code word—your secret signal that all is, in fact, well. "Hi, this is Bob Smith and my code word is 'tree'—nope, there's no fire here—no need to call the fire department. Thank you."

As a security expert, I've seen bad guys exploit the notion of a code word time and time again. Let's take a straightforward home invasion, and not even one that turns violent. Criminals assumed the home was empty because lights were off—lo and behold, half of the family is on a vacation, and Dad is watching TV on the second floor. He pushes the panic button and runs down the stairs to see what's going on. Not so fast, say the bad guys. When the alarm company calls to check in, they force him to say his code word. An alarm code word is great when things are fine—but it can be weaponized against you as a crime unfolds.

Situations like these are why putting *in writing, in your alarm security company file,* the concept and clear directions for "callbacks and rings" is paramount.

Let's say the crime I described above is in motion. You've just acquiesced to the intruders' request to save your life—you gave the alarm company your code word . . . you said it over the phone, in your voice. But all is not lost. Why? You've explained to your alarm system company that whenever you give your code word, they need to call back in exactly five minutes (or however many minutes you put in your instructions) and that you'll pick up on or before the third ring. If the alarm company does that and *you* do not pick up at the time and ring designated, then they know you are in significant trouble, and they will alert the authorities.

As for the bad guys? They will either pick up the phone on the incorrect ring or assume that since you gave your code word, they're in the clear. You, on the other hand, will feel a surge of calm and protection when you hear that callback. You'll know to leave it ringing, signaling your distress. If the criminals tell you to pick it up, pick it up after your designated number of rings have elapsed. Unlike a code word, there is no way after that point, under any circumstances, that your alarm company will think that you're safe.

And if it is all an accident? When the alarm system's representative calls you after your puppy bumps into the panic button, simply stay at the phone after you've given your code word. When they place their "designated callback," pick up at the right time.

Tailor this concept for you and your needs. Maybe your "call back and rings" is ten minutes, ten rings." Maybe you give them a second code word at that callback to indicate that you're truly safe. Maybe you tailor a "distress word" with them so that if intruders do make you pick up your phone during the company's callback, you can signal to them that all is not well. Make your distress word believably unobtrusive in the course of small talk. Let's say it's "wire." "Hi guys, a wire must have tripped in the system. Everything is totally fine here." Click. The police are on their way, and the bad guys think the dogs have been called off.

There is a way to reverse engineer this as well—again, do what you feel works best for you. The same concept—you've given your code word—but instead of the company calling you in, say, three minutes, *you call them* within three minutes. This can be as simple as you hanging up after the code word is given, and then immediately picking the phone back up and calling them. This method is especially workable if you call with a second code, and two codes are noted in your file. Tell your company: *My first code word is*

"California." Then, I call you within five minutes and my second code word is "Arizona." If you do not hear back directly from me within five minutes or I don't say "Arizona," you know I am under duress and that you need to send help.

Weapons

If you have a firearm in your home, it needs to be locked in a safe, with its safety on at all times. I was in the FBI for years, I am comfortable around guns, and I respect gun ownership, but this point is nonnegotiable. Locked up with the safety on—no exceptions. That said, when you need it, you need it, and you need to be able to access it in seconds. Without any children in the home, practice opening your safe and removing the safety as often as possible, so that if you ever need your weapon, it can be of use to you.

NINJA TIPS:
EASY ACTIONS FOR A MORE SECURE HOME

Save Your GPS

Closest emergency veterinarian, closest hospital, closest police station, so you can get there immediately in an emergency. If you're not proficient or comfortable with GPS, drive the routes a few times to get comfortable with them in a crisis.

Dispose of Trash

Show me the garbage, I'll show you the person. Be sure to fully destroy any trash involving junk mail, your family's prescriptions, or debit and credit information. Armed with your birth date, gender, and name, you'd be amazed at what an identity thief can access.

Update Garage Door Codes

Change the code at random intervals, and never leave the factory code as your password.

Let Trusted Neighbors Know About Vacation

Make arrangements with your trash, mail, and delivery services with that neighbor alone—it's never a good idea to alert multiple companies that you won't be home when you call to pause services like a newspaper or your mail.

Lock Your Door—Always

Whether running out for a quick cup of coffee or just walking the dog around the block, always secure your home when you leave it. If you have an alarm, it's only as good as your remembering to set it . . . and test it regularly!

STREET SMARTS: CARS AND GATES

Car in the Driveway

If the whole family's inside watching TV with the volume blasting, an experienced thief can access your glove compartment in a matter of minutes. Never leave purses, shopping bags, or valuables in view when your car is parked, and make sure to always, always lock your vehicle, even if you predict you'll be back in the driver's seat in a matter of minutes.

Gated Communities and Crime

Let me start by saying hat I have absolutely no problem with gated communities for what they offer and afford a person seeking safety and security. The problem I do have with gated communities is the specific mindset that some people have around them: "I live in a gated community, so I don't have to do anything else." OK, so, unless you can tell me who in your community is a professional thief, who's addicted to drugs (and therefore needs money), you still cannot forget, either consciously or unconsciously, to keep up with your safety and security. Are they more secure? Maybe. But in every set of statistics, there's an outlier.

COP CRIB NOTES:
WHAT DO LAW ENFORCEMENT PROFESSIONALS DO TO TAKE HOME SECURITY TO THE NEXT LEVEL?

"Strong Room"

Choose one room in your home and install interior locks to create a "strong room." In a worst-case scenario when you cannot exit the home, you can retreat to this safe room and lock the door and call the authorities. Buying time in a dangerous scenario is key. You'd be surprised what a difference thirty to sixty seconds can make when whatever it is a bad guy is planning to do could take your life.

People go to varying degrees to create these rooms, but it can be as simple and as inexpensive as a closet you can lock from the inside.

Camera Apps

You've all seen the commercials for these—let me tell you why these could save your home's security. You're on vacation, let's say, in Florida, for New Year's Eve. A deliveryman, whether he has ill intent or not, comes to your door and rings the doorbell. You can see him and talk to him from your phone, and critically, *he does not know that you're not home.* In 1980, if no one answered a door after a few attempts, word might spread that it was a solid target for a burglary. That no longer needs to be the case. Anyone coming to your door can see your face, whether you're in Tokyo or in the bathroom. You can also see them, which is a huge security advantage. Do they look trustworthy? Today, every American has the opportunity for state-of-the-art home security.

Know the Distance of Your Closest Helpers

When we do home security assessments for ultra-high-net-worth families, one of the things that we've found to be very valuable is to figure out first responders' response times.

Everyone should know response time for local first responders because it can affect how you react to a crisis: How far away is my nearest fire department? Nearest police station? Nearest hospital? If fire trucks are twenty minutes away, you might not want to stay in the home and try to battle the flames yourself after calling 9-1-1. The smoke inhalation alone would be life-threatening.

And by the same token, let's say your spouse is having a heart attack. If the nearest ambulance is forty-five minutes away, you might rethink waiting for an ambulance to transport your loved one to the hospital. But if paramedics are two minutes away, it would be foolish to load a person in distress into your car.

Neighborhood Airhorn Agreement

Consider buying an air horn for your own home and your neighbor. The deal is: If you hear this air horn, call 9-1-1 and direct first responders to the house. The added benefit is that the noise could scare off a bad guy. The good news is that an air horn is going to attract a lot of attention. And at an hour like 2:00 a.m. or 3:00 a.m., people are going to hear that and know that something's up. An air horn can be purchased at any hardware store.

High-net worth home security suggestions

▶ Do not draw attention to wealth or lavish spending in public photographs or write-ups, whether that be on Instagram or in a newspaper article on your attendance at a charity dinner that costs, say, $10,000 a plate. These glamorous images attract bad actors, all while matching your face to your name and indicating your income level and your whereabouts. Beyond petty theft or burglary, it is scarily simple to use this information to triangulate an email address and devise an email blackmail scheme. Closely guard your personal info!

▶ Create "crisis packages" for each family member for use in a medical emergency or when a family member is missing. (And hey, families of any income level can also create these packages! I like keeping one package for each family member in a clear sandwich bag.) The packages should include:

- [ ] Recent, realistic photo

- [ ] Fingerprints

- [ ] Emergency contact information

- [ ] Photocopy of passport

- [ ] Pertinent info on any medical conditions, allergies, or immunizations

- [ ] A DNA sample (optional)

▶ Consider installing a gate that can block cars at the entrance to your property. Establish a "family policy" on how often you will change the gate's passcode, and who has access to the code.

▶ Conduct a background check on every person who will work on or in your home—plumbers, electricians, caretakers, etc.

▶ Install CCTVs or app-based cameras at every residence door, garage door, and property entrance.

CHAPTER TWO

Home Safety

The Key to Protecting Your Family Is Planning

BUT WAIT, YOU'RE THINKING—didn't we just go over this in "Home Sweet Home Security"? Not quite. Home Security tackles bad actors attempting to gain access to your home, while "Home Safety" addresses accidents, pitfalls, and lack of preparedness with no ill intent, whether it be a hurricane, shoddy workmanship on a staircase, a fire, or even how to prepare against a sunny day at the home pool going terribly wrong. Since safety issues are much more commonplace than those people who'd want to do us harm, I'd venture to say that this is the most CRITICAL chapter you read in the whole book. If you read just one part of *Prepared, Not Scared*, make it "Home Safety."

Let's start with medical emergencies. They can strike day or night, at home or on the road, and there's no bad actor in sight.

What matters is: Do you and your household know how to react? This chapter arms you for every possible situation.

STANTON STORY

EXERCISING MY WHOLE LIFE, it was a great day when I got the opportunity to work out with body-building legend Bill Grant. While I was able to keep up in the amount of weight we were lifting, I couldn't keep up with the unique angles Grant could reach with those same weights. The next day, I felt an odd and totally unique soreness. I complained, stumped, and a loved one recommended I go to the doctor's, since I was no stranger to workout pains, and this felt totally different.

The X-rays were done, the doctor gave me a pass, and I assumed everything was fine. I got in the car the next day, excited to continue the epic working-out sessions.

Not so fast. I got a call on my cell en route to the gym, and my life was completely turned around: This was urgent. I needed to turn my car around and get to a radiologist, stat.

That radiologist told me I had a tumor the size of my fist on my lung. Never in my life having smoked, done drugs, or done steroids, I asked, "Why me?" What went wrong here? I asked the doctor if I was a dead man walking. He put his hand on my shoulder and said, "I'm very sorry—is there anyone I can call for you?" The writing was on the wall. This wasn't just a medical emergency, it was a death sentence.

Well, I'm still here, and this is where the serendipitous, fickle finger of fate steps in. One of my regular training partners at the gym is a guy named Raja Flores—a Lebanese-Cuban, as if his name didn't tell you as much. He just happens to be a world-renowned thoracic surgeon. Let's just say, it's good to have smart friends in places that face life-or-death situations every single day.

Now, while I'm convinced that this was a slow-burning medical emergency, it was on fire nevertheless, and I'm convinced it could have been avoided with better choices—though I'm not a doctor. (Less sugar, less stress—you get the picture.) That said, I felt secure, figuratively and literally, putting my heart in Dr. Flores's hands.

This chapter will diagnose the most common medical emergencies that hit everyday people, and how best to avoid them, with expert advice from some of the best doctors around.

HOME MEDICAL EMERGENCIES CHECKLIST

☐ Do you have CPR and Heimlich maneuver directions and kits easily accessible in your home? Many families print out and tape the directions inside their kitchen cupboards.

☐ Do you know how to identify different types of burns and how to be the "first responder" for a burn in your home?

☐ Do you have in your first aid kit . . .
- ► Naloxone?
- ► A finger pulse oximeter?
- ► Bacitracin and neomycin gels?
- ► Aspirin?
- ► Gauze?

☐ Do you have in your home . . .
- ► Multiple working fire detectors?
- ► A carbon monoxide detector?

FAMILY PLANNING

Have a family plan of what to do, and practice going through different scenarios with your entire family. Far from scaring your children, this will empower them, calm them, and give them confidence. I can remember the renewed sense of control and confidence I felt after I went through this with my mom and dad at age eight.

Fire

We will use steps and tips from the National Fire Protection Association nonprofit service. Their site—http://www.nfpa.org/public-education/by-topic/safety-in-the-home/escape-planning/basic-fire-escape-planning—is thoroughly comprehensive, especially for families that include children.

Family Emergency

Getting sick at school

Reassure your child that he or she should go right to the nurse when they're feeling ill—you won't be mad, their teacher will always say yes, and the nurse will be able to make them feel better faster than if they keep sitting at their desk, hoping for their ailment to go away.

In the age of cellphones, I've heard and seen firsthand that many young children, cellphone in hand (or pocket), will ask to go to the bathroom, text a parent, nanny, babysitter, or family member, and ask to be picked up.

Do not encourage or support this in your child. Children are ignorant of the ways in which many symptoms can point to larger problems, and therefore bypass an entire support system when they go to the bathroom with a cellphone over visiting a certified nurse with a degree. That headache could be meningitis; that stomachache could be appendicitis. Avail yourself of the experts, and teach your children to, too.

Don't be afraid of encouraging your children to involve trusted adults by requiring that they go to the nurse when they feel sick—I know of many youngsters who have "faked" an illness to get out of class. One of three things was inevitably true: They were being bullied, they were far too smart for their class, or they were far too behind in their class—all conditions an experienced nurse will be able to convey to the parent. Again—so much more helpful than your child texting you from the bathroom.

Younger sibling is injured in the care of an older sibling or vice versa
Present the children with an already fully formed plan on what to do if their brother, sister, or friend gets hurts while they're playing.

If they have a cellphone, this could mean calling you, or calling 9-1-1. If they don't, encourage them to knock on the door of the most trusted neighbor (or store counter, if you live in a city) for help.

Discuss with the children scenarios for which it would be appropriate for one child to leave the other—for example, Johnny has broken his leg falling out of the tree house and can't walk—so Tommy is allowed to leave him to get help from a trusted adult.

What if an injury strikes when no one your child knows is anywhere near them? Teach them about adults who are trustworthy more often than not, and how to spot and approach police officers, security guards, or even a parent or a nanny with a brood of kids.

A babysitter is acting inappropriately
From drugs or alcohol, to sneaking a boyfriend or girlfriend into the home, to stealing from Mrs. Robinson's jewelry box, my private

clients have seen it all—and since children always observe more than we think they do, they can see this behavior and be afraid to report them to you, since they recognize their sitter as an authority.

Before a sitter even comes over, lay down some ground rules, and later, tell your child that just like you have rules for them, you also gave rules to your sitter:

- ▶ "I'd like any of your phone calls to be less than fifteen minutes, please."
- ▶ "Please don't have any friends (or boyfriends or girlfriends) over when we're gone."
- ▶ "Would you mind staying out of our bedroom? It probably wouldn't come up, but I'm wrapping some presents for the kids and I don't want them to see them."

    (Then, lock the door to your master bedroom. If you don't have one, install one. While most bedrooms don't feature locks that can be secured from outside the room, this is a crucial final deterrent from burglars while you're away on vacation, or even at work for the day. Start the habit of viewing your bedroom as an "apartment" within your larger home that needs to be secured.)
- ▶ Give your children, as well as your babysitter, your cellphone number, as well as the landlines to the restaurant or friend's home you plan to visit. Assure your children that you'll answer any call or text if an "emergency" is taking place—good scenarios to run through include a babysitter unable to wake up or unable to be found in the home.

A sudden power outage, when family members are at different ends of the home—or parents are away

Choose one central room in the home that you'll all move toward, and stick to your plan whenever this happens. Then try to fix the problem.

Quickly and loudly identify yourself and the issue to encourage both calmness and action. "Hey guys, I'm in my bedroom, and I think using the hairdryer blew a fuse. Let's all meet in the family room."

Home Invasion

Emphasize to your children that, while this scenario is rare, working through possibilities will ensure that everyone will act more calmly if criminals break into your space.

Again, your children will probably be less scared of this than you are—kids tend not to overthink things and are comforted by the thought of camaraderie and shared plans.

EXPERT INTERVIEW
Dr. Raja Flores

What are the most common injuries you've seen sustained in the home?

So, something like this, it depends on whether you're talking about kids or elderly people—because that's certainly what I see in the emergency room as the groups that get hurt at home. With children and the home, your top worry—and prevention efforts—should circle around them getting their hands on, and then drinking, toxic substances, like bleach or lye.

Another big thing with kids is firearms. You have to make sure that any guns in your home are locked—accidental use of a firearm is a big cause of injury for kids.

Choking is another one. Every adult should know and have experience in performing the Heimlich maneuver. In houses where there are pools, drowning needs to be a concern—especially if toddlers are around.

Also, believe it or not, suicide is on this list. It's one of the top killers of older kids, along with drunk driving. Of course, drunk driving happens outside the home, but sadly, an attempted suicide of an older child or teen is a medical emergency I've seen with a rising trend—I've tragically seen this as young as twelve.

But back to the elderly—the other age bracket that I see getting injured at home. Everyone laughs at this because they know the saying, but it couldn't be more true: "Help, I've fallen and I can't get up!" Just a simple fall can cause hip injuries, wrist injuries— and actually, many times it comes from slipping in the shower. (Make sure that you always, always, always have rubber traction stickers in the bottom of a shower that an older person is using.) The same goes for step stools in a kitchen or pantry—many times, an older person was simply reaching for a can of soup, and they fall and break a rib or a hip. If you have an older person in your life, encourage them to ditch the stools and small ladders and keep everything in their home on a reachable level.

The same goes for stairs. Is your family in the habit of leaving things on the stairs? Well, then, you have to stop, even if there are no elderly people in your home—I've seen the injuries. Many households now have multiple generations—that means that just as the older folks are getting susceptible to bad falls, toddlers are leaving toys around. Be careful, be mindful.

A safety button, worn around the neck, can literally save a life. An older person, especially if he or she lives alone, has to be able to get help, and quickly. We've had patients who come into the ER after lying in their house alone for thirty-six hours. In some tragic cases, those same patients have died not from the fall, but from the lack of water or kidney failure that results in not being able to move for hours on end.

But young adults and middle-aged people are far from exempt when it comes to the potential for a major accident at home. What do Americans this age try to do? Fix their homes. From gutters to roofs to renovations, there's a massive probability that you're not taking the right precautions, let alone avoiding the potential for injuries. So often, the guy in the emergency room I'm treating was just trying to clean out his gutters. When in doubt, hire a professional, and put your own safety first.

Smoking, beyond that it's bad for your health, has a hidden danger for the elderly: falling asleep when smoking can quickly mean third-degree burns, if not a house fire. Smoking is a very common cause I see in the emergency room of third-degree burns and injury in older patients.

Try to start thinking of injuries and accidents in the home as age-related—different ages are prone to different emergencies.

What are the top medicines every family should keep in their home all the time?

I think the main thing to stock up on first stems from this extreme question: What can I have in my house that ensures no one who visits me is going to die on my watch? What is the most lifesaving drug, and what's the most life-threatening situation that you can find yourself or one of your kids' friends in? What could happen right in your home, and you might not even realize what's happening? The answer: a deadly allergic reaction.

Many times, throughout a lifetime, you don't know you're allergic to something, or you may end up developing an allergy to something. So epinephrine, or an Epi-Pen, is a huge item at the top of this list—I make sure to always have one in my home—and so should every family, whether they have relatives with allergies or not. You never know who could visit your home and suffer an attack, and you can never know what allergies your loved ones could be developing over time. We've seen firsthand how epinephrine can stop or slow an attack. Along those same lines, I would also have Benadryl in your home.

About eight years ago, completely unbeknownst to me, I was living with an allergy to the medicine ibuprofen, which I had developed as an adult. So what happened when I took a simple Advil? My mouth swelled up and I couldn't swallow. Thank goodness, in the same medicine cabinet, we had allergy medicine, and I could reach for it and take it immediately.

I recommend calling your children's pediatrician, explaining that they have many friends over to the house frequently, and that you're worried that any one of them could develop an allergy or have an allergy that you don't know about, and that you'd like to have a prescription for an emergency Epi-Pen for your home first aid kit. (Some parents even keep a second injector in their car.)

On a separate note, let's tackle an issue just as deadly, and just as shocking when you're faced with it. With the trends in patients I'm seeing in the emergency room, you want to consider having a prescription filled for medicine that counteracts illicit drug use, and keep it permanently in your home. Hand in hand with America's opioid epidemic, I encourage everyone to keep naloxone in their homes. According to the National Institute on Drug Abuse, most pharmacies will sell naloxone to you without your having to obtain a prescription when you describe that you want it in case a family member, friend, or visitor is in danger of overdosing on heroin or even a prescription opioid. This "anti-drug drug" is available as a nasal spray, an injectable with a needle, or an "auto-injectable" that will literally voice instructions to you as you attempt to save a life—much like an automatic defibrillator machine. Now, buying naloxone may sound drastic to you—and I understand that feeling. But I've seen it all, and you'd always choose to be ready to handle any situation that you find yourself in. Since drug addiction is often hidden by its sufferers because of intense stigma, trust me, users' identities will surprise you. Be prepared, not scared.

Finally, is anyone is your life in danger of a heart attack? Then I recommend asking your doctor if keeping sublingual nitroglycerin in your home is right for you. This is an extended release pill that you can put under someone's tongue when they're suffering from (or you suspect they could be experiencing) a heart attack.

What about first-aid items in the home? Does everyone really need gauze, medical tape, and all the supplies we learned about in high school health class?

Again, in the pharmacy aisles, look for what could save a life. Here's a first-aid item that everyone absolutely needs, but it's so easy to forget because it's far from glamorous: bacitracin and neomycin gels. You probably know these as Neosporin, or a triple antibiotic ointment. I've seen seemingly minor cuts and scrapes become full-blown, even life-threatening infections because they weren't immediately treated with an inexpensive, over-the-counter antibiotic.

Keep aspirin in your home. It can reduce fevers and take away minor pains and aches, so why not have a constant supply?

This will seem high-tech, but it's very worth it: a finger pulse oximeter. (Yes, you see this in the movies whenever someone's in a hospital bed!) This clamp costs less than $15 at Walmart.

If someone in your home gets a severe injury, has a heart attack, or is quite simply extremely sick, place this on their index finger to get a sense of their pulse and how much oxygen is moving through their body (above 96 percent is normal . . . 70 percent is approaching cardiac arrest). If your loved one can't speak, isn't cogent, or you just need a sense of what's happening, this handy tool not only tells you exactly how dangerous the situation is, it's an easy statistic to relay to paramedics when they arrive in a harrowing emergency. For example, it's more effective to tell 9-1-1, "She's been throwing up all day, and her pulse is slowing—her oxygen's also been going down for the last few minutes so I thought I'd call for an ambulance," rather than, "My daughter's sick, I'm not sure what's happening, but it seems like she's falling asleep on me here." If you're prepared (but not paranoid), so are the first responders arriving at your home.

From a child gushing blood from a gash on a table corner to your grandmother experiencing a stroke, this tiny, inexpensive tool is something every home should have.

Let's move on to the more obvious items. Yes, every first-aid kit needs tweezers for splinters, gauze, medical tape, and something that you can make into a tourniquet. You'll often hear that tying or buckling a belt works. It's true that it helps, but you might be better served by buying an inexpensive tourniquet online or in a pharmacy.

What are the most common mistakes you've heard of people making when a medical emergency happens at home?

These are simple. Not getting to the ER in time, not calling 9-1-1 in time—when in doubt, call. It's better to pay the ambulance fee and know you made a mistake than to lose a loved one or unknowingly worsen their condition with your hesitation.

When it comes to at-home injuries, you wouldn't believe the number that result from drinking too much. If someone is inebriated and drifts off, turn them on their side. Doesn't matter which side—just not flat on their back. And as always, when in doubt—or if someone's not waking up—never hesitate to call for help.

This isn't so much a mistake as a silent killer resulting from a lack of preparation: carbon monoxide poisoning. Make sure your home has both fire detectors and carbon monoxide detectors, and be sure to always turn off your cars, stoves, and any other appliances that burn gas. It sounds obvious, but don't rule out creating a nightly checklist of rooms to go through—including the garage—to confirm that everything is "off."

What's the best way to prevent medical emergencies at home?

This is so simple, but you'd be amazed at the number of households that don't check this off the list:

- ▸ Install a working carbon monoxide detector.
- ▸ Educate yourself and your family on what to do if an emergency strikes.
- ▸ Install multiple working fire detectors.

Short and sweet. Do these three things, and you're on the way to staving off a tragedy.

So given that, should families have a home medical emergency plan?

Yes, absolutely. I tell everyone: The first step of every plan is calling 9-1-1. The reaction is usually, "Well, of course I know to do that!" But I always go back to that great Mike Tyson quote: "Everyone has a plan until they get punched in the mouth." Without getting too graphic or upsetting, think about it: Could running to the phone, dialing three numbers, and explaining the situation be your first and fast reaction if your child cut a finger off while helping you cook? Fell off their bike and you suddenly saw exposed bone? Visualize it, and visualize running to the phone. If you've ever experienced a fraction of witnessing a loved one get hurt, you know what I'm talking about. It can be hard to put a thought together, let alone dial numbers and make a call.

So, how do you start helping despite the walls that shock can put up? The answer is simply family meetings, early and often. Review different scenarios, and practice them as a family. Firefighters come to grade schools and tell kids to do this with their loved ones, and many families both come up with and practice a home fire plan. Do doctors come to grade schools and tell kids how to set up a family medical emergency plan? No, but they should. I'd venture to say that medical mishaps are more common than house fires.

If you're not prepared, you're not going to react appropriately. You're just not. So, go through what happens if someone falls, incurs a life-threatening allergic reaction, or has a heart attack, and go through your steps and roles as a family.

After you call 9-1-1, and until the ambulance arrives, I always say the best medicine you can give is administered by ear: words of comfort. Why? As the initial first responder and witness, consider first and foremost why it's so important to calm the patient down: blood loss increases with a quickly pumping heart (and the pulse would be extremely heightened if someone knew they were hurt.)

But how do you calm them down?

Touch, touch, touch. Human contact can lower stress, and therefore, the pulse. You should take deep breaths, tell the patient to take deep breaths, and above all, project that you are calm and that this emergency will be taken care of quickly and correctly—even if you're acting. Your patient will react to and mirror your reaction, especially if you're dealing with a child. Repeat constantly that an ambulance is on the way.

When a trauma victim enters the emergency room, nurses and doctors speak lowly, slowly, and calmly, right next to a patient's ear. If they are having trouble hearing because of shock, speaking close to the ear is essential. Projecting calm is key.

Should families have a pediatrician on speed dial? Is this better than calling 9-1-1 in some cases?

This is something you can truly tailor to your own family's comfort level, and I've seen people use either option first with success. If two adults are present, one adult should call the pediatrician, and one adult should call 9-1-1 at the same time.

In a single-adult home, if the child is somewhat comfortable, and this injury is not immediately life-threatening, a pediatrician can be a huge help, and sometimes, simply calling a pediatrician to check in is sufficient. The same goes for what I call "chronic exacerbation of an acute condition": for example, your child has been diagnosed with strep throat, and it seems to be getting worse.

For excessive bleeding, an allergic reaction, or if you sense that the child's life is in danger, call 9-1-1.

Dr. Flores is the Mount Sinai Medical Center Department Chair of Thoracic Surgery. After earning his medical degree from the Albert Einstein College of Medicine in 1992, he pursued his general surgery internship and residency for five years at Columbia-Presbyterian Medical Center. His cardiothoracic surgery residency was spent at Brigham and Women's Hospital, Harvard Medical School. He also holds a master's in biostatistics from Columbia University. He has led a number of major studies, including research on the effects of asbestos on mesothelioma. Dr. Flores is a world-renowned surgeon and researcher in his field.

NOW, ON TO FIRE SAFETY. Did you know that each year, nearly two thousand home fires in America lead to fatalities? On top of that, seven thousand additional fires lead to serious injuries.

STANTON STORY

L et's chalk this one up to the shoemaker having holes in his shoes! It was Christmastime and I was in a festive mood—like most people this time of year. I decided to light some festive candles around the house. I was warned not to, for that common fear of "burning the house down." After roaring that I am the king of my castle, and that I'm well equipped to blow out candles before I go to bed, I got back to watching Ebenezer in *A Christmas Carol*. Fast-forward—I got back to watching John McClane blow things up in *Die Hard*—required viewing for every Christmastime in the Stanton household.

Boy, was I wrong. Let's take a look at the facts before I tell you what happens next.

BUT FIRST, YOU NEED TO KNOW . . .

WHAT ARE THE TOP CAUSES of accidental home fires?

- ▶ Cooking is the leading cause of home fires and home fire injuries.
- ▶ But smoking is the leading cause of home fire deaths.
- ▶ Heating equipment is the second most common cause of home fire fatalities.
- ▶ The takeaway? Cooking causes injuries, but the risks resulting from smoking and heating equipment are far greater.

HMEP: YOUR HOME MEDICAL EMERGENCY PLAN

Write in the book, then photocopy and post in a highly trafficked area of your home. Practice, practice, practice.

HELP

WHO?	WHO IF?
1. Who calls 9-1-1?	a. As a household, we've decided that _____ (1a) calls 9-1-1 if someone has a medical emergency.
2. Who administers words of comfort? This cannot be the same person who calls 9-1-1.	b. As a household, we've decided that _____ (2a) will comfort the person experiencing a medical emergency.
3. Who calls 9-1-1 if _____ (1a) is not home or is the person in trouble?	c. As a household, we've decided that _____ (3a) calls 9-1-1 if _____ (1a) is having the medical emergency or is not at home.
4. Who administers words of comfort if _____ (2a) is not home or is the person in trouble? Remember, this cannot be the same "Who If?" who calls 9-1-1.	d. As a household, we've decided that _____ (4a) administers words of comfort if _____ (2a) is having the medical emergency or is not at home.

MONITOR

WHO?	WHO IF?
5. Who takes notes, mental or actual?	a. As a household, we've decided that _____ will take note of what happened to the patient and what's happening to the patient.
6. Who finds the finger pulse oximeter and puts it on the patient's index finger during a home medical emergency?	b. As a household, we've decided that _____ will grab and place the finger pulse oximeter.
7. Who takes notes, mental or actual, if _____ (5a) is the patient or not home?	c. As a household, we've decided that _____ will be our "Who If?" in this situation.
8. Who finds and places the finger pulse oximeter, if _____ (6a) is the patient or not home?	d. As a household, we've decided that _____ will be our "Who If?" in this situation.

EXIT

9. _____ (2a or 4a) continues to offer words of comfort to the patient as they're taken to the hospital.

10. _____ locks the door to the house.

11. _____ drives the household members who can't fit in the ambulance to the hospital.

12. If _____ (2a or 4a) is the patient or not at home,

_____ continues to offer words of comfort to the patient as they're taken to the hospital.

13. If _____ (10) is the patient or not at home, _____

_____ locks the door to the house.

14. If _____ (11) is the patient or not at home,

_____ drives the household members who can't fit in the ambulance to the hospital.

PRACTICE

Remind your household: When the time comes, you might not be able to think clearly. That's why we go through the motions.

For our first practice, _____ will pretend to experience a medical emergency.

As a household, we've decided that _____ will grab and place the finger pulse oximeter.

_____ will lead the practice session. If our practice leader isn't at home on practice day, _____ will lead the practice session.

If our medical emergency pretender isn't at home on practice day, _____ will act out a medical emergency.

SIGNED

_____   _____

_____   _____

_____   _____

The peak months for home heating fires are December, January, and February.

The top three days for home candle fires are New Year's Day, Christmas, and New Year's Eve.

But don't forget fires outside—children playing with fire leads to dozens of deaths in America each year. Another interesting fact—federal research refers to this as "youth fire-setting," which is scarily prevalent in children ages six and under.

And knowing all this as a security expert, what did I do? Back to the Stanton story:

Fast-forward to 2:00 a.m.—when I wake up thinking I need to lower the thermostat. Everything is in a dark fog as I try to look for the time on my VCR (remember those?). Exhausted, my head goes back down on the pillow, which, in retrospect, could have been a fatal move if I hadn't awoken, minutes later, due to the heat.

Feeling a palatable weight all around me, through the dark, I slowly make my way through the bedroom, and finally into the living room, where I was greeted by eight-foot-high flames hitting the ceiling in my co-op. The source? The lovely candle display I insisted upon lighting earlier.

Fortunately, I had a big pot of water from making pasta for dinner earlier that evening. Luckily, that doused the flames. The moral of the story? We're all from the planet Earth, not the planet Perfect, and we're all susceptible to making mistakes.

FIRE SAFETY CHECKLIST

☐ Do you have at least one smoke alarm and one fire alarm on every floor of your home, including in the basement and the attic?

☐ All right, you have smoke alarms. But are all of them less than ten years old? They should be.

☐ When you light candles, do you make sure that adults —not kids— blow them out before leaving the room?

☐ When an appliance's electric cord is broken or frayed, do you throw the item away immediately?

☐ Here's one you might not have thought of: Do you clean your dryer of lint after every use? The U.S. Fire Administration reports that nearly three thousand home fires and five deaths are caused by dryer fires every year. The typical culprit? Lint.

☐ If you have children in your home, are matches, lighters, any flammable fluids, and yes, even candles, locked away? Children's curiosities can lead them to attempt to start fires long before they've been taught safety precautions.

☐ The National Fire Protection Association (NFPA) recommends that you create a home fire escape plan and identify two possible escape routes out of each room in your home, whether it be a window, a door, or moving to another room. Draw a floor plan of your home and map out escape routes using the template on page 88, courtesy of the NFPA.

☐ Call it the rule of two: Your family's fire escape plan should be practiced twice a year. So, two escape routes discussed from every room, and two practice sessions each year. By the way, your practice should end, of course, outside the home at a meeting place you've agreed on. Growing up, my family's was a tree across the street.

How to make a
Home Fire
Escape Plan

Memorize your fire department's emergency phone number and write it below:

_____

The Official Sponsor of Fire
Prevention Week Since 1922

- Draw a floor plan or a map of your home. Show all **doors** and **windows**.
- Mark **two ways out** of each room.
- Mark all of the **smoke alarms** with Ⓢ. Smoke alarms should be in each sleeping room, outside each sleeping area, and on every level of the home.
- Pick a family **meeting place** outside where everyone can meet.
- Remember, **practice** your plan at least **twice a year**!

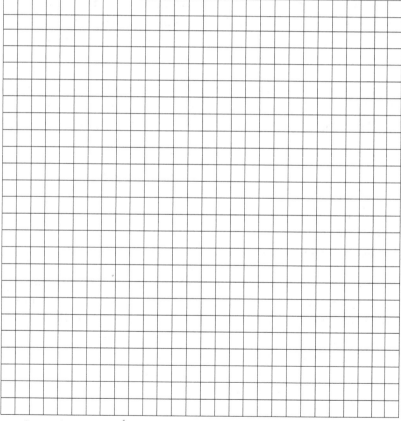

Grown-ups: Children don't always wake up when the smoke alarm sounds. Know what your child will do before a fire occurs. Get more information on smoke alarms and escape planning at **www.nfpa.org/factsheets**.

Sparky is a trademarks of NFPA. ©2017 NFPA

Diagram courtesy of the National Fire Protection Association.

HOME POOL SAFETY CHECKLIST

DROWNING IS THE NUMBER ONE CAUSE of accidental deaths in children from ages one through four. Not firearms, not car crashes, not kidnapping, not choking on food. Here's a fact that surprised even me: More than half of drowning deaths of children ages one to three occur in residential settings. If you do the math on the national statistics, that means that more than 150 children under age five die from drowning in a residential pool setting every year. That's just one small part of why it's paramount to take pool safety very seriously.

Before we go over our checklist, let's take a look at just how dangerous pools can be:

- An average of 5,600 pool- or spa-related hospital emergency department visits for nonfatal drowning injuries occured each year in 2013, 2014, and 2015. And these numbers only reflect ER visits for children ages fifteen and under!

- An estimated average of four hundred children die each year from pool accidents, and there's no one age group that sticks out here—so it's important to stay vigilant well into the teenage years.

- For children fifteen and under, there are about twice as many drownings involving boys as involving girls.

So now, to our checklist . . .

☐ No child should be able to gain access to a pool without an adult opening access for them. That means a fence, and a highly placed, complicated, childproof lock. If an adult isn't in the pool area, that gate needs to be locked—and the fence needs to be taller than the children who might use the pool.

☐ Pool alarms are a relatively new technology and a fantastic, lifesaving idea. The idea is that if someone falls into the pool, an alarm in your home goes off—so you are alerted and can take action.

☐ Make sure your pool covers are up to date and that no child could fall through them or wriggle under them into the water.

☐ Store any portable pools while they're not in use. Children can fill them and fall into them when not supervised.

☐ Call your local first responders or law enforcement departments to ask what the local and state statutes say about pool safety. Some states, for example, have laws around types and heights of pool fences.

HOME POISONING SAFETY CHECKLIST

FORGET THE CHILDHOOD memories of big scary stickers on your mother's cleaning sprays—when a child or adult is accidentally poisoned, it's much more statistically likely to be from something innocuous lying around your home. According to Safe Kids Worldwide, nine out of ten poisonings occur at home.

Let's take a look at the leading causes of poisoning in children . . .
- ► cosmetics and personal products
- ► cleaning supplies and laundry products
- ► pain medication
- ► the metals or sealants in toys, coins, and thermometers

And now, leading causes of poisoning in adults . . .
- ► pain medication
- ► sedatives, hypnotics, antipsychotics, and antidepressants
- ► cardiovascular medication
- ► household cleaning items
- ► alcohol

Not exactly out of a sci-fi movie, right? So, here's what you can do to keep your home safe from chemical accidents and poisoning:

☐ Keep household cleaning products locked away from children.

☐ Check with your home's previous owner about whether lead paint was used anywhere in the house. If it was, be sure to quickly vacuum up or dispose of any paint chips that fall on the ground. Children can put these chips in their mouths, leading to health problems.

☐ Keep all medications locked away from children.

☐ Save the toll-free Poison Help Number (1-800-222-1222) in your mobile phone and share it with any babysitters or visitors. Two million people call the line every year, so you're not alone.

STANTON STORY: *Extreme Weather*

THE YEAR WAS APPROXIMATELY 1989—at my age then, I got what I felt was an offer I couldn't refuse: running security for one of the most famous nightclubs to ever put up a velvet rope: the China Club. They were opening a satellite club in Aspen, Colorado. The one catch? I had to decide whether I would take the job, and then get there within forty-eight hours. As far as I was concerned, there was no decision to make. This young man was going west! Besides gasoline, the first thousand miles were run on pure adrenaline—and I had thirty-six hours to get there after I made my decision.

By the time I got to Denver, I was still excited, but I'd been up for twenty-four hours straight and was exhausted, but no less enthused. When I stopped in a gas station for directions (this was before GPS and cellphones), the locals were telling me I should wait until tomorrow to make the drive—a winter storm was coming in. I looked out the window and saw snow flurries, and I remember laughing and saying to myself, "You ain't from the Bronx—this ain't shit"—too young, too dumb to know what was yet to come.

About halfway through my 150-odd-mile drive from Denver to Aspen, I drove right into the center of that extreme storm. On my path were cars and trucks that smarter drivers had abandoned to take cover.

My Nissan Pathfinder, while great on South Bronx side roads, in this storm had no more grip than when I tried to run across a skating rink in my sneakers. I remember pulling over and thinking, "Am I going to die here?" I was afraid of keeping the car on and suffocating from lack of oxygen—but conversely, I was afraid of turning the car off or the engine freezing, and dying from hypothermia.

So, what did I do? I pulled over, and I alternated. Heat on, heat off. [Thirty years later, I found out that ready.gov actually does recommend you stay in your car if trapped inside during extreme weather!] The moral of the story? Respect Mother Nature (always), as well as local wisdom—listen to the old-timers in any gas stations you may drive through.

OK, what do folks who live in coastal areas and homeowners who live in the Great Plains have in common? They all face extremes by potential natural disasters: hurricanes, earthquakes, tornadoes. You need to be prepared.

Do your own cost-benefit analysis. Call your local power and light company and ask them, "What was the longest period of time the power has gone out in this area?"

If two days straight is the longest span (across the last fifty years or so), determine: Can you go two days without power? If not, buy a generator. If yes, don't buy a generator. Then, make sure you have food and bottled water for two days.

If you don't want to go six hours without power, buy the generator. Then again, if you can go six hours, don't buy it. It's about how you feel.

People think, "It won't happen to me" but we always put on our seat belts. So, without a deep dive into the destruction that extreme weather can unleash on your home (we've all seen the news reports), here's a checklist that will ensure heightened safety in any home across the country.

EXTREME WEATHER SAFETY CHECKLIST

☐ Do you have enough bottled water and food (that doesn't need to be cooked) for the longest recorded length of a power outage in your area?

☐ Keep at least one mobile phone fully charged so you aren't dependent on a landline for emergency phone calls.

☐ It sounds old-fashioned, but I recommend keeping one battery-powered radio around to listen to weather alerts and updates in the event of all phones and electricity dying. The National Oceanic and Atmospheric Administration (NOAA) has a 24/7 free radio service where you can hear everything you need to know. You can look up the stations here: http://www.nws.noaa.gov/nwr/.

☐ Call your local first responders (yes, I say this a lot throughout the book—communication is so often the very basis of safety!) and ask how they plan to react to and warn about extreme weather.

☐ NOAA and its website, weather.gov, will tell you that being underground is the safest place to be during a tornado. Make sure everyone in your household knows they need to quickly get to a storm shelter or basement if a tornado is close.

☐ Many homes don't have basements or reinforced shelters. If you don't, your job with this checklist is to list a few places where you can secure yourself instead. Some ideas? A bathtub or shower, a crawl space, a space under stairs, a closet, or even a hallway at the center of your home. Make sure to close all doors to block flying debris.

☐ If you're in an apartment building and high winds strike, get to the lowest floor possible—ideally the basement.

☐ Flooding can erode the structural integrity of your home, and it can also lead to drowning. If you fear your home is flooding, do not stay inside. Create a plan with a friend or relative nearby, on higher ground, and leave your home if you have to.

☐ With the different regions of the country, the changes in global weather patterns, and the different extreme weather that can occur, I can't recommend enough checking out https://www.ready.gov/severe-weather to personalize your household's extreme weather checklist.

A Note on My Checklists

Remember—it's important to complete every item on these checklists, but I don't know your exact personal situation—there may be items that your local first responders suggest you add. So, as always, I suggest that when you move, or, hey, if you've been in the neighborhood for ten years, call up your local first responder departments, tell them you have a pool, tell them you're developing a family fire safety plan, and ask them what they recommend.

CHAPTER THREE

Your Personal Safety

Self-Defense and When to Use It

WHILE THERE ARE MANY DIFFERENT TYPES of "crimes" on the books and varieties thereof, there's one thing I can virtually guarantee all survivors have in common: When they all woke up that particular day, none of them had a clue they'd be a victim, or they'd take steps to avoid becoming one to the best of their ability, and as much as the circumstances would allow.

If you're reading this now, congratulations on the inclination you've shown so far in taking control of your own personal safety, and the safety and security of your loved ones. While good Samaritans are good, you'll never know if they'll be around when your number is up, and getting your own shit together and becoming your own personal protection specialist/bodyguard is better than hoping for the best!

You may have seen some of my examples on TV of what I like to call "Social Experiments" (NBC's *Today* show and *Dateline* are but a few), when I put people to the test to see their best.

Unfortunately, most failed ... miserably. Cultivating situational awareness and honing critical thinking skills will only enhance your confidence and exponentially lessen the chances of ill intention doing any harm if it comes your way. The ironic part of it is that once you get proficient at this way of thinking and acting, you'll never know what troubles you may have avoided. With a few changes, the potential predators will pass on you, seek weaker sheep, and recognize your inner LION.

Subtopics:
- ▶ Identifying the threat (threat assessment)
- ▶ Stalking
- ▶ Harassment
- ▶ Mugging
- ▶ Assault
- ▶ Physical Confrontation: when to fight, run, or just play dumb

Self-Reflection: Be Real

Think about how you would truly and honestly react in an attack situation, with no ego. Could you really punch someone, or would you freeze?

Like a surfer, see a wave of trouble coming at you, and make adjustments to how you need to ride that wave. When you're out on that ocean, there is no magic to suddenly decide, "I don't want to be here." Decide how you'll ride out a bad wave before it happens.

Handle things correctly—and by that I mean only do what you are comfortable with. Do you want to appease your assailants and calm them down? Or do you want to be aggressive and scare them off? There's no wrong answer. Whatever gets you out alive and safe is what you need to do. There is no right answer, either, because no one can see the future in an attack, even with hindsight—you are dealing with an unpredictable, and likely highly unstable, person. You did not choose this wave.

To do your best mental and physical preparation for a physical threat, you need to assume that in a personal physical attack, you will freeze. You need to assume this for two reasons: This is how most people act, and this is the worst-case scenario.

Remember, there are multiple options available to you in a frightening situation:

▶ Watching a sad situation that you're not immediately involved in: You can call the police, alert them to what's going down, and choose to intervene at your own pace. You can also leave, and contact help from another place.

▶ Fourth of July Party: Two men are drinking heavily and arguing over the Super Bowl. You have a bad feeling that this could move into a brawl quickly. Not exactly an action movie scenario, but: You can leave. You don't need to stay and "fix things." Not your job. Your job is keeping your family safe.

▶ Nightclub: In the heat of a brawl, chairs are flying and your friends are on the other side. Use your critical thinking. You've hopefully committed to seeking out situational awareness, and you know where the exits are. Threat assessment should tell you there's a chance you could get hurt, especially since the alcohol flowing at these places can cause someone to take out a gun or a knife. Leave through the side exit.

We live in a tremendously politically correct world. Why didn't you jump in and help? Why did that person creep you out? Are you a bigot because you moved away from someone on the subway?

So, how do you defend yourself and keep your reputation intact?

You channel your inner bodyguard. Your most powerful weapon is your mind. You are a badass when you know how to handle a situation. First, the best way to win a fight is to avoid it. If you feel all efforts to avoid that scenario have been exhausted, and you're on that wave and you can't get off, fight to win. Fight as if your life depends on it, because it does.

Identify your assailant, for both your safety and for the police later:

- ▶ Clothing: Where can you tear? What can you tell the police later?
- ▶ Height: Where will my punch land on this person? What can you tell the police later?
- ▶ Getting Away or Staying: Can you run faster than your assailant? Or do you have the actual long-term training and muscle mem-ory to stay and fight? Decide before it happens.

Growing up in the Bronx in a working-class area of diverse nationalities, it was inevitable that you got into fistfights—just human nature, especially as kids. I got into a scrap and got a bloody nose—I shook hands afterward in some cases, and then I kept playing whatever I was playing. It helped me learn to defend myself physically, but also how to use humor and street smarts to get out of fights.

When I ask my friends with kids now, "Have your children ever gotten into a fight?," they literally clutch their chest. We live in a world where the principal calls you into school if your child didn't invite one classmate to their birthday party.

I bring this up because, less and less, children don't grow up learning to defend themselves. And that's fine—maybe we're all getting better at living together as a society, and getting kinder. But my point is that you still need to know how to defend yourself, because the bad guy coming for you sure does.

And that assailant is counting on you to be not only offended (and thus mentally knocked off balance), but to be frozen. Self-defense classes, situational awareness, and research will thaw that natural-reaction frozenness, and even spark the fire that will better your chances of safety and survival in the face of violence.

STANTON STORY

BEFORE WE GET INTO REAL-WORLD, step-by-step tips, let me tell you about a time when I feared for my life.

For many Americans, the idea of proactive personal safety protection is little more than having ten-year-old pepper spray at the bottom of their bag or saying they've taken a few months of karate at the local YMCA. Suffice it to say, in cases like these, numbers are your best friend . . . practice consistently, and learn the statistics of becoming a statistic, and localize these numbers for your town and your workplace.

For me, safety and security have literally become my life, and this next story could have easily ended my life—so I still think of it constantly.

It was around 2006, and I'd just signed a contract with NBC to be their very first safety and security contributor on the *Today* show. It was a BIG deal for me, and I was riding high. On this particular day, I had a late-afternoon shoot (no pun intended here, I swear) with some time to kill.

Being crazy about movies, I decided to go to a matinee, and *Mission: Impossible III* was my film of choice. Since it was midday, the movie theater had only about thirty people, so I thought myself lucky to nab a seat center aisle, center row. It was going to be a good day, or so I thought.

As we thirty lucky Tom Cruise fans got just about halfway

through the movie, a classic confrontational scenario happened—and not on the screen—this was in real life.

Sitting one row behind me and several seats to my right, loud, loud chatting starts up. "So man, the rims on this car was soooo sweet! Damn homie, Lil Z had to cop me those wheels!" Yep, it was a guy jabbering on his cellphone, right in the middle of the movie, right in the middle of the theater! So, what to do, what to do?

It's at this juncture where, for you to understand where I am in the cultural landscape, I need to properly explain what happened next. Being born and raised in the Bronx is best described as a unique experience. To put it mildly, folks from the Bronx are quite passionate and not shy about expressing their passions/opinions/anger.

With that being said . . . WARNING: DO NOT TRY THIS AT HOME . . . the following was done by a trained professional . . .

This dude keeps jabbering away as if he's home on his living-room couch! So, I go through my own personal checklist . . .

▶ I could get up, look for an attendant, and ask them to do the dirty work, but the guy would probably know it was me.

▶ I could just leave, of course, but hey! I'm really liking M:I:III.

▶ I could move my seat. This option, in all candor, is the option I advise all reading this to take. But similarly to the shoemaker with holes in his own shoes, I did not take my own career expertise to heart.

▶ I could ask him to stop, please. (Spoiler Alert . . . This should be everyone's last option, but of course, the first one I went with.)

Back to the scene where we last left jabber-jaw. With a grand gesture, I throw my right arm over my seat, twisting my upper torso in his direction, and not saying a word, just stare at him. I hoped he would suddenly become self-aware and hang up (another Spoiler Alert here: People who are already annoying you in public are usually not capable of self-awareness about whatever they're annoying you with). But, just like the quintessential busy waiter, he refused to make eye contact and continued on with his animated conversation. After watching and listening for about twenty long seconds, I say in a low, steady tone, "You've gotta be kidding me."

With that, he hangs up the phone. EUREKA! Against my better judgment, option four of my checklist worked! Or did it?

Not so fast—my plan "worked" for three seconds, because about three seconds after I watched him hang up, he stood up and started "mother-***ing" me louder than the dialogue between Tom Cruise and Philip Seymour Hoffman. Soon, this guy is telling me how he's going to "f*** me up." And to make matters worse? His buddy stands up beside him.

Now I have two guys, over six feet tall, telling me how they're going to come over and kick my stupid ass. (OK, they didn't really say "stupid," but I added that myself, because speaking to this guy in the first place was extremely, extremely, stupid.) So, what comes next? They're threatening to come over and play proctologist with their Timberland boots, I decide to stay seated, utter not a word, keep my right arm still hanging over my seat, and I slowly wave them to "come on." I offer them the old "bring it" hand motion, all while smiling, no less!

OK class, can someone tell me why I did this?

Was it because I thought I was a badass?

Was I looking for them to hit me so I could press charges and then also sue them in civil court?

Was it because I was not only listening to their words, I was also watching their body language, and I surmised that in this scenario, the best defense is a good offense?

Keep in mind: It is an irrefutable fact that even Super-Semi-Top-Secret-Ninja-PI-Gunslinger-Spies like me aren't perfect, and I should have just walked away initially. But hey, in life, we will all dig ourselves into messes, and we need to quickly decide which ladder to use to effectively climb out of our messes.

In this case, I chose a verbal ladder by going with choice number three, with the mindset that offense is sometimes the best defense. By egging these two idiots on, I gambled and won, figuring they'd be all show and no go.

Regardless of my various other skills, if they'd physically engaged me, I was determined to use a combination of verbal and nonverbal judo, situational awareness, critical thinking, along with knowing the cultural landscape of a matinee movie theater in the heart of New York City to help me out of this mess (hey, as any New Yorker will tell you, and I should have known, don't go to a movie in Manhattan if you want it to be a few hours of quiet contemplation). Thankfully, the only fights taking place were on the movie screen, and not in front of it.

I tell you this story to reiterate that we're all from the planet Earth, not the planet Perfect. Is it acceptable to politely ask someone who is talking in a movie theater to be quiet? Yes. Should you be able to without fear of physical violence? Yes. But that's not always reality.

Knowing your landscape and how to escape various scenarios to keep your personal safety and security intact is what this chapter is all about. Being able to bench-press over three hundred pounds, enacting your Second Amendment rights when confronted with deadly intent, or having a black belt in karate is fine. But why not learn, if you can, how to use words and critical thinking to avoid taking those steps? Having a black belt in B.S. (Bill Stanton, I mean) takes only the cost of this book and the time it takes to read it. And did I mention? No violence needed . . . unless you're comfortable using it.

BUT FIRST, YOU NEED TO KNOW . . .

IN THE UNITED STATES . . .
- ▶ There is an aggravated assault every forty-one seconds.
- ▶ There is a murder every thirty-four minutes.
- ▶ There is a rape every four minutes.
- ▶ There is a robbery every two seconds.
- ▶ Violent crime is showing signs of RISING—and increased in 2015.
- ▶ Firearms were used for every seven of ten murders, 41 percent of robberies, and one in four aggravated assaults.
- ▶ The global homicide rate is fifteen times higher than terrorism's death rate.

EXPERT INTERVIEW
Dan O'Connor

MR. O'CONNOR IS SO KNOWLEDGEABLE, and his level of experience coupled with a willingness to speak out is so rare, that I couldn't put him in my book just once. Here's what Dan has to say about personal safety and security when you're outside your home.

Take a Self-Defense Course

Just as important as telling you what you should do, these courses will tell you what you shouldn't do. These courses will also tell you where to hit. You would be amazed at what a simple hit, punch, or kick can accomplish. These courses are especially effective at explicating different tactics for males and females—no matter the identity of the victim or the perpetrator.

Take a Self-Protection Course

Going beyond personal self-defense, these can help with your home and even your driving security.

If you're a woman, and you're attacked . . . go for GET: Groin, Eyes, Throat.

Groin

Needs no explanation. But if you don't do this quickly and precisely, directly into the organs, you might lose your moment to take down your assailant if you miss, thereby wasting energy. Many women over the years have been told to "go for the groin." That's true, and it's often effective, but don't go for the groin at the cost of causing an injury that's more lethal or more quickly delivered. In short, don't waste time thinking, "I have to wait to deliver a blow until I have a clear shot to the groin."

Eyes

Forget the pain felt by the eyes—self-defense experts have been advising survivors to go for the eyes for decades, if not centuries, because of one simple human reflex: hands. When your eyes are in danger, it's our human instinct to drop what's in our hands and move our hands toward our eyes. If your assailant is holding a gun or a knife (or even your purse), you have a better chance of getting him to drop it if you go for his eyes rather than going for his hands.

Throat

A swift jab to the throat can be lethal.

Daniel O'Connor is the founder of The O'Connor Group, a company that offers international security solutions. Dan's career has crossed decades, continents, countries, and cultures. He worked for the CIA from 1979 to 2005, serving as the chief of personal security for the last five CIA directors and their deputies. He has also served as the CIA's chief administrator of U.S. facilities in Europe, as well as Central and South America.

TIPS AND TRICKS

CARRY A BOGUS WALLET if you move through a highly trafficked or claustrophobic area.

Make a log of occurrences that strike you as "off."

Build a case—there's nothing pleasant about this, and it's not going to feel warm and fuzzy. If you want courts and policemen to take you seriously, the sad fact is that you often need written or graphic documentation(smartphones come in handy here!). A fact of law enforcement taking a threat seriously is: Documentation changes things. If law enforcement is not helping or cannot help you, discuss the occurrences with a lawyer and consider asking them to send the person who you perceive to be threatening your safety a cease and desist letter. By the same token ask the lawyer if a cease-and-desist letter could potentially trigger escalation of the upsetting behavior. They will have a body of work, if they've dealt with issues like this before, that should point you both in a helpful direction.

Insure Your Jewelry

If someone wants something in order not to take your life, or if you have an opportunity to extend the time of your bodily safety, you don't want to hesitate. Insuring your jewelry, especially the pieces to which you have emotional attachment, will help you cut down that hesitation time. "I wouldn't hesitate!" I can hear a few readers grumbling. Trust me, when panic sets in, you might move more slowly than you ever thought possible, and a few seconds could make the difference.

Your Most Powerful Weapon is Your Voice

You might feel terrified to "draw attention" to the situation, but statistics show us that with yelling, a criminal backs off. A thief trying to score doesn't want to run into people inside a home—and they don't want to draw attention to themselves in robbing a mark out on the street. Chances are, not only will they back off, but good Samaritans will approach the situation, coming to your aide. Sometimes, an approaching person more than anything else will prompt the criminal to take off.

It Sounds Silly, But Scream "Kee-yah"

It's a hokey exclamation we've all heard in cheesy martial arts videos, but a physical assailant will hear the term and immediately question whether he chose the right mark. The term denotes training, and no attacker wants to go up against someone trained in any type of self-defense. If you can muster the word in a convincing way, it can't hurt you to use it. Furthermore, self-defense is all about buying yourself time. I've seen in my own training that "Kee-yah" can cause milliseconds up to full seconds of paralysis—if only because it raises questions.

NINJA TIPS FROM DAN O'CONNOR: BEFORE YOU'RE ATTACKED, READ THESE QUESTIONS

WHEN UNDER ATTACK or duress, ask: Who are you dealing with? This will help determine how you should operate.

Sane or mentally ill?
If your attacker appears to be not of sound mind, consider . . .

▸ Talking down, appeasing.
▸ Summoning your empathy for the mentally ill, offering help.

Remember, they could be speaking to someone who's not there. If they start engaging with that person, that is good for you.

A mentally deranged person will often fight beyond their limits and fight hard because they have no sense of inhibition or reason. They are not inhibited against breaking their arm—they are not registering pain the same way a sane person would in that moment.

If you have options, you do not want to get into a physical altercation with a deranged person. Option A should always be getting away.

Remember, a sane person's logic does not apply for someone who's deranged.

NINJA TIPS: IMPROVISED WEAPON
AND YOUR BODY AS A WEAPON

FITNESS IS ONE of the most lucrative industries in America right now. Chances are you work or live near a pretty inexpensive gym. Use it! Learn how to throw a punch with defensive authority. You don't need to be Bruce Lee to defend yourself. It only takes . . .

- five pounds to break a nose
- six pounds to break a collarbone
- a quick "spear hand" in the neck to put someone on their knees.

If you're walking, running, or working out alone, be very aware of your surroundings. Consider using just one earphone and texting a friend beforehand about where you're working out.

Weapons That Aren't Guns

- Break a plate or a glass: You have a knife. An unbroken, circular plate thrust into a neck can bring an assailant to the floor.
- Cellphone: If you're smaller, a cellphone can be a better weapon than a fist. Grab it in your hand and swing it toward the assailant's face.
- A table, couch, or desk is a barrier between yourself and a knife and some bullets.

Remember my tip that it only took five pounds to break a nose? By the same token, any object can become a weapon. In distress, look around you and move your hands for anything you can grab. Any weight in your hand adds to the force of your punch.

STREET SMARTS:
USING MAPS TO YOUR ADVANTAGE

THE MOST RELIABLE PERSON to count on for your safety is you. It is so empowering to learn more about your surroundings. Don't hesitate to look at maps or blueprints before you go somewhere new.

BAD GUY POV: WHO ARE THEY LOOKING FOR?

To SCORE A STEAL or even use more evil intentions, I'm looking for a small young woman with her face in her phone, earphones in, and she's had a drink or two. Let's talk first about the scary fact of the matter—in your lifetime, you will likely experience an assault or invasion of your personal space against your will. The stats you read on page 105 are from reported crimes (where someone got police involved), and we know for a fact that most crimes go unreported. Why? The Justice Department has two sets of statistics—one from police, and one from normal folks. When people have the freedom to talk casually about what's happened to them, we get a better idea of how many painful instances have actually occurred—and sometimes they double what's told to law enforcement.

EXPERT INTERVIEW
Sam Arrowood

What can you tell us about violent crime?
I'm a retired deputy sheriff, and I investigate a lot of violent crime in a town of about forty to fifty thousand people—we're in rural western North Carolina, close to Asheville and Charlotte.

The most helpful lesson I've learned over the years is that nobody's immune to violent crime. Yes, there's always that potential
that there are safer areas than others. But the world we live in
today means that terrible things can happen anywhere, even in
small towns. Leaving any upward or downward crime trends out of
it, seemingly random events strike every demographic—which is
why situational awareness is so key.

Like you might have a fire extinguisher or a spare tire, I recommend having some sort of weapon in your home. You might never
need it, but if you need it just once, it could save your life. Do what
you are comfortable with, but remember that in so many crisis situations, you will need to rely on yourself for your own protection.

***Let's say you're pulled over for a traffic ticket, or you've been
blamed for a more severe incident. How should you, if suspected, act with law enforcement?***
It all goes back to respect on both sides, from both sides. Ninety-nine
percent of the time, a police officer is a dedicated professional.
Talk to your children about being cautious but respectful from
an early age. If an officer senses aggression or evasion, and the
subject could be completely innocent, chances are, their antennae
go up. Your first reaction should be to calmly diffuse and de-escalate
a situation. Unfortunately, we see lack of respect on both sides,
which can escalate tension.

What's your first piece of advice if you're being assaulted?
Run. Don't be afraid of employing situational avoidance—it
doesn't make you a chicken. Criminals and predators love darkness and isolation. Knowing that, there's no need to shop for
groceries at three o'clock in the morning. If you see one car in the
parking lot, consider coming back later.

In a surprise attack, men especially find themselves in situations where culturally and psychologically they might not want to run away—bad idea. There's no such thing as settling things with a few punches these days; either you're going to be outnumbered because it's a set-up, practiced crime, or someone is going to break out a weapon.

Staying and fighting, for anyone, should be a last resort. My suggestion is to fight for your life, because you are. Realize what's happening, and fight until you can run away, and then run away.

The world is not all good, and that's not negativity on my part—it's just a fact. There are evil people, and there will always be evil people, in this world. You have to prepare yourself, mind, body, and soul, to deal with that.

Retired McDowell, North Carolina, county sheriff Chief Deputy Sam Arrowood has been in law enforcement since 1984. Today, Arrowood teaches law enforcement at two of his local community colleges, including course work on police's communication with the public and reacting to and working with mentally unwell suspects. He brings to the table decades of experience in investigating and responding to violent crime.

Better Securing Your Home

YOU KNOW, across my decades of experience, I've found that having a dog is really helpful. I've interviewed hundreds of thieves, and on more than one occasion they've admitted that they avoided homes with a large dog, or even a little dog because it would make a lot of noise and draw attention to the situation.

As with everything, I say that with door locks, you get what you pay for. Buy a high-quality lock that will slow down the intruder long enough for you to either escape your home or grab a weapon.

Remember, your phone is one of your best options for a weapon. Arm yourself with your phone. Call 9-1-1. Your door lock should be strong enough that you have the time and the edge to do that.

To be a victim of a violent crime is very rare, but if it does happen, it can become the most devastating event of your life. So to mitigate that harm, it doesn't hurt to prepare yourself with the level of training you're comfortable with. Something I'd like us to consider is how much time young, impressionable children are taught about fire safety—what to do in the event of a fire. But what are we teaching them about what to do in the event of violent crime at home?

EXPERT INTERVIEW

Dr. John Spears

How can a firearm owner, a normal person with limited experience, ensure that they can use a gun, when threatened, and use it confidently?
The old saying is that buying a firearm does not make you ready to defend yourself, or even safe. Getting *trained* does.

So the number one piece of advice is that you *must* seek competent training, always.

To bring in aspects from our other experts—when it comes to home defense, it's crucial to have a plan and that everybody in the family knows the plan. Where are we going to go? Are we going to retreat somewhere? Who's in charge? Who makes any outgoing calls? (Is it a set person?) All of those things are going to be critical to making sure a terrifying situation unfolds for the innocent parties with the greatest levels of safety and security.

All correct. The head of the household can't be the only one who knows what the plan is. Home invasion awareness starts at the most basic level with awareness of physical security. Is everyone in the home in the habit of locking doors, closing gates, and closing windows? Are the heads of the household checking the physical security of the home every night before the family goes to bed?

But *everyone* in the family can help by being aware of the most simple things that you have to get into the habit of doing, like locking doors behind, closing garage doors, closing gates, simple things like that. Those basic actions would frequently deter the vast majority of criminals who would try to invade your home.

Beyond that, having a plan and *actually discussing it*, and even better, rehearsing it with your family, is the only way to even begin to ensure that everybody knows what to do in a crisis. Everyone in the family should know that they have the ability and that they are imbued with the responsibility to call 9-1-1 if there is an emergency.

Many times, even in the workplace, employees will defer to the boss to decide if there is a critical situation occurring. Every person should have the individual initiative to know that, if there is a dangerous situation developing, you don't have to wait for some-body else to give you approval to inform law enforcement through the 9-1-1 system. Law enforcement would *always* rather evaluate and intervene in a situation that turns out to be a false alarm made in good faith, than miss a dangerous situation. Waiting until the dangerous situation has developed to its peak before calling 9-1-1 is always a worse plan than calling early on.

Right. And I think in some ways, that's just workplace psychology. You're waiting for your boss to tell you to do so many things, that, unfortunately, we can slip and stay in that mindset when an emergency takes place. That reminds me that for families

*with children, it's helpful to tell them, "When it comes to calling
9-1-1, that's something where you never need to ask my permission,
or come find me and ask me if you can call the number. Just
call it." And that can be taught as early as you're teaching your
children basic safety drills.*

Every child, whether he has just learned how to dial 9-1-1 or is a
teenager, needs to know that he does not need to seek permission
from the parent or the authority figure to call the police if something dangerous is happening. If a stranger is breaking into the
house, a kid doesn't have to ask his parents if it's OK to make a call.

We want to teach our children to be independent, and to be safe,
and to think for themselves, and to take responsibility for their
own safety, but it's natural for all of us—it's the default position, if
you will—to look to somebody else to tell us what to do in a critical
situation. As much as you can explain that default mindset to your
household, and explain that the mindset needs to be pushed away
in an emergency, the more you are moving toward a strong sense
of security.

People can be naturally afraid that they're going to get in trouble for calling the police. Again, police would rather be called to a
false alarm made in good faith than miss a true emergency.

How do you recommend firearms be secured in the home?

My personal opinion is that all firearms need to be locked in
some kind of secure container—a gun vault is best. If not a gun
safe or a vault, then a locked room or closet that can be secured. If
it cannot be secured in a vault or locked room, then a trigger lock
should be applied. And most important, a loaded firearm should
never be unattended by the owner. *Any time* that pistol is not on
your body, it should be locked up.

Leaving a loaded firearm somewhere in the house while you

are working out, or you're mowing the lawn, or you're tending the pool, or digging in the garden, where anybody—your child, your child's friend who is over playing at your house, or someone you don't know—could come upon that firearm, you need to know that YOU have just created a potentially unsafe situation.

So again, if you're going to have a handgun that you carry for self-defense, any time it is not on your body, it needs to be secured.

The most common way to do that these days is with a small single handgun vault that can be accessed by a digital code or by biometrics. These can keep anybody but you from accessing that loaded firearm.

On that note, without giving away state secrets, can you tell us any pieces of military-grade advice for using a firearm in a high-stress situation?
It's all fundamentals. The four fundamental rules of firearm safety apply EVEN in a gunfight:

- ► We treat every gun always as if it were loaded.
- ► We never point our weapons at anything we don't intend to destroy.
- ► We never put our finger on the trigger until we make a conscious decision to shoot.
- ► We are always sure of our target, and what's beyond it, and what's between us and our target.

So, even in the most terrifying encounter you could imagine, you still need to be using those fundamentals that you learned when you first picked up a gun—and those in the military are using those four fundamentals as well?
Yes. We never violate the rules of firearm safety, from as high-stress a scenario as a gunfight down to heading home after battle, and whether the group is two or three people, to a full infantry

company, we never violate those rules. The number one rule
among them: Treat all weapons as if they are loaded.

We never violate those rules, and all of our training emphasizes
ways of moving around partners, moving through structures
and buildings, moving to contact, without ever violating any of
those rules.

One of the very interesting things about those four fundamental
rules of safety is that in most cases where there is a tragedy, if even
one of those rules had been followed, there likely would have been
no opportunity for a mistake to be made and for somebody
to become unintentionally injured, or worse.

Understanding that every person is different, and that some
people need more training than others, let's say you're a woman
who has never been in the military or a man who has never
been in the military. How often should that person be training
with their handgun they keep in a small gun safe, solely to
defend themselves in the event of a home invasion? How often
should they be taking that handgun to a firing range and
practicing with it?

After you've gained some basic competence in, primarily,
manipulation of the weapon, how to handle it safely, and in basic
marksmanship, the vast majority of training can be done without
live ammunition and can be done in the home.

The most important part of safety and ability with a firearm
like a handgun is in familiarization and the ability to manipulate
it correctly.

That means having the empty, unloaded, cleared pistol in your
hand, in a safe place in your house, with no ammunition in the same
room where you're training, and practicing dry firing, pulling the
trigger, aligning your sights, and maintaining good control of the

weapon—all the fundamentals.

If you carry from concealment, this practice might involve drawing the weapon from concealment, and that could also mean dressing the way that you would normally dress as you would go through daily life. Helpful training can also involve practicing accessing your firearm correctly and safely.

If you were doing that for ten to fifteen minutes a day, over the period of a month, you would then most likely have a skill set developed where you would be able to practice it *weekly* and maintain those skills. Then, if you could make it to the range on a schedule in which it was reasonable for you to do so you'll consistently, you would find that the majority of all of the skills that you need could be developed without ever using live ammunition.

And it's probably safer, and more secure, to keep live ammunition away from your training, depending on your comfort level. It's removing a variable.

The majority of your skills with a firearm don't involve you having to pull the trigger on live rounds. The majority of the skills that you need, especially early on, can all be developed by becoming familiar with how to manipulate the firearm correctly. Live fire is of course necessary, but it is not where most of your early skills will be built.

John Spears, D.O., is an orthopedic spine surgeon with extensive military background as a former medical sergeant in the United States Army Special Forces.

BAD GUY POV:
WHY YOU NEED A FLASHLIGHT
IF YOU HAVE A FIREARM IN YOUR HOME

A HANDHELD FLASHLIGHT is a really good idea because it allows us to look at something without pointing a gun at it. There are major issues to consider before entering a confrontation, including whether or not you've got other family members in the house, confirming the intruder is really a threat, and whether or not it would be better to put yourself in a position of advantage behind cover. Verbally challenging a potential assailant, giving him the opportunity to leave, is the first choice. Candidly, your life's going to be so much simpler if you don't kill someone in your house. It's a terrible, litigious, traumatic situation even if you were completely and totally justified both legally and morally. Some home owners have been cleared criminally in the death of intruders only to be pursued in the civil courts by the family of the deceased. One night when someone else was in the wrong turns into years of trauma for the person who acted within their rights.

CHAPTER FOUR

Staying Safe in the Workplace

How to Avoid Danger on the Job—
from Harassment to Terrorism

IT'S CALLED THE RAT RACE for a very good reason. Every day across the country millions of people (primarily between the hours of 8:00 a.m. and 6:00 p.m.) are rushing to work, working at work, then rushing home from work.

It's the in-between time at our collective workplace factories, cubicles, malls, restaurants, and warehouses that things rev up. But do they always? Many times, our workplaces become an extension of our homes, for some a more intimate or comfortable place than for others. Often, the busy people of America bring personal letters, bills, and other personal items into their office. Others will shower or stay late into the night, sometimes sleeping there.

My point is: Are you aware of precautions you would take in case of emergency—especially to the same extent that you've planned for your home? What about if a fire breaks out? Workplace violence? Or is it just about making it to the water cooler to discuss *Game of Thrones* and indulge in office gossip? (Yes, a little tough love there.) Most folks will offer (when pressed) that their level of situational awareness and strategic planning for facing a workplace emergency is passive at best. Most workplaces will offer the practice of a monthly fire drill, or display with simple maps the keen knowledge of the back exit (known by some as the perfect getaway for sneaking out early on casual Fridays).

This chapter offers you the opportunity to up your game at work. Here, you'll enhance your skill sets with statistics and expert knowledge, gaining a better understanding of what to do in an area where most don't know what to do. For right now, you might not be the supervisor, foreman, manager, or team leader at work (and congratulations if you are!), but you can become the CEO of preparing yourself for whatever comes your way on the job.

STANTON STORY

As I'VE SAID TIME AND TIME AGAIN, it's been my observation and experience that we treat two places like an extension of our home: our cars and our workplaces. Unfortunately, I had to learn the hard way why you should not do that.

It seems like a lifetime ago now, but I vividly recall key moments of my life as a young cop in uniform at the Fortieth Precinct in the South Bronx, where gun runs were as common as coffee runs for civilians. Because crime and the danger level were so high, one had to really fully give their trust to their brother and sister officers in blue. We became a family, and, like families do, we called our shared building—in this case the Fortieth Precinct offices—"the House." Sharing meals, working out together, and locker room chatter—the homey nature of the place was infectious.

But it was in that locker room where I, and so many others, felt so comfortable that trust betrayed us. We would get undressed, hang up our gun belts and all our gear after a tour of duty, and hit the showers. Since we did feel like the Fortieth Precinct building was an extension of our homes, we rarely locked our lockers when we showered or were called briefly away.

It wasn't until a brother officer's gun was stolen that we became keenly aware that, even though we were all cops, this is by no means home. Treat your work like your work. The station house isn't in fact our house, but a workplace—and it was a rude awakening. As some Americans have sadly experienced, yes, cops can be criminals!

It was a cop who went rogue, stealing his partner's gun and a police radio to go do armed robberies as his second job. The lesson here? Be prepared, not scared. While it's great to trust folk (and maybe you don't want to work a job if you can't seem to trust a majority of your colleagues), never forget what can happen. Your actions and inactions have consequences.

Without further ado, let's take a look at how you can keep yourself and your belongings safe and secure at work.

BUT FIRST, YOU NEED TO KNOW. . .

Fire

U.S. fire departments respond to a non-home building fire once a minute across the country.

- ▶ Four Americans will die in fires at their office and forty-four Americans will be injured in office fires each year.

- ▶ Just one-fifth of these fires burn on weekends, when offices are nearly empty, which means . . . you guessed it . . . these fires are mostly sparked by human error.

- ▶ U.S. fire departments respond to an estimated 14,500 workplace fires in high-rise buildings alone each year.

Bomb Threats

Of the nearly two thousand bomb threats across America annually, schools, offices, and businesses remain the most targeted by those threats year over year. High schools and department stores, believe it or not, receive the large bulk of these threats.

Shootings

- ▶ Seventy percent of the active shooters strike at a commercial business or school, and active shootings appear to be increasing every year.

- ▶ If an active shooting is unfolding, chances are extremely high that the perp is a young male acting alone.

- ▶ These shootings start and stop in the blink of an eye. Seven in ten ongoing shootings last five minutes or less, and nearly half are over in under two minutes.

► The scariest fact uncovered by the FBI in all this? Sixty percent of the active shootings end before the police can even arrive.

Cybercrime

Back in 2005, most U.S. businesses survived a cybercrime against them every year. As technology advances, these crimes are constantly intensifying. Take the following as a wake-up call to your new normal—a sobering recent report from *Fortune*:

The latest statistics are a call to arms:

► According to Cisco, the number of so-called distributed denial-of-service (DDoS) attacks—assaults that flood a system's servers with junk web traffic—jumped globally by 172 percent in 2016.

► Cisco projects the total to grow by another two and a half times, to 3.1 million attacks, by 2021. Indeed, the pace of cyberassaults is only increasing.

► Internet security firm Nexusguard reports that it observed a 380 percent increase in the number of DDoS attacks in the first quarter of 2017 compared with a year earlier.

Illness

Every year, three million private-industry employees are injured at work or get sick from their work . . . so, if you're a working full-time in America, that means there's a 3 percent chance your work will wind up hurting you.

When it comes to the physical structure of your workplace, "fall protection" is the most frequently violated OSHA standard—in other words, can your floor and your walking space safely hold everything that's moving across it each day?

Trouble with the Boss

Putting physical danger aside for a minute, we all know that the day-to-day grind is taxing under the best of circumstances. But what if your boss is the absolute worst? A recent study out of Great Britain shows that employees under abusive bosses can not only become depressed, but are also more likely to take on undesirable behaviors at work.

Relationships with same-level colleagues offer no guarantees, either. A 2012 CareerBuilder study found that more than a third of workers say they've been bullied at work, and nearly one in five of those employees say their health has suffered as a result.

Workplace Violence and Harassment

What is the most prevalent type of workplace violence?
Well, it varies by the profession. According to OSHA, taxi drivers are most likely to be murdered on the job—at a twenty-times-higher rate than other workers.

Healthcare workers, teachers, lawyers, and those who work in media are especially prone to experience on-the-job violence.

What are some warning signs of workplace violence?
You might think it won't happen to you, but it absolutely could. Each year about two million Americans report violence at work—and those are just the ones who report it. According to the National Safety Council—an organization that acknowledges there's no foolproof way to prevent or predict an attack—here are behaviors that could precede violence:

▸ Drug or alcohol abuse
▸ Paranoid behaviors

- ▸ Multiple days off and declining performance
- ▸ Comments on suicide, or sudden withdrawal or depression
- ▸ Emotional responses to criticism
- ▸ Multiple complaints about perceived unfair treatment
- ▸ Disregard for company policies
- ▸ Beyond intentional violence, over four hundred Americans are killed each year in work-related accidents.

BAD GUY POV: BEHIND THE SCENES OF GENDER-BASED HARASSMENT

DON'T ASSUME SUING YOUR COMPANY is on the table. According to estimates, sixty million American workers, perhaps unbeknownst to them, have signed arbitration clauses in their employment contracts, which means that any complaints taken seriously will play out in arbitration, not in the courts. In some cases, the arbitration payout is roughly ten times less than compensation that results from open court.

Gender-based harassment doesn't need to mean that sexual activity is involved. According to the Equal Employment Opportunity Commission, "Harassment does not have to be of a sexual nature and can include offensive remarks about a person's sex. For example, it is illegal to harass a woman by making offensive comments about women in general." So let's say a coworker constantly says, "I'm so sick of mothers breastfeeding at work. Everyone knows they're taking time off in that break room and not working as hard as the rest of us." That's harassment.

If someone knows they're upsetting you, and they thrive on the power rush from that, chances are they will continue unchecked.

Roughly 75 percent of those who participated in an EEOC survey said they had been harassed at work but did not report it to a supervisor. That's a harrowing thought when, according to the EEOC, about 25 percent to 85 percent of women report being sexually harassed at work at some point over the course of their careers. The game plan for many men and women is too avoid bringing attention to an already stressful situation, and endure, endure, endure.

But how can we change that? How can we make sure our civil rights are fully protected at work?

After what you've just read, there's every reason to throw up your hands and leave your office . . . but if you're staying (whether for love or for money), this chapter will show you that just a cursory know-how in office safety and security could save your job . . . or your life.

EXPERT INTERVIEW
Jessica Ramirez

Let's talk about bullying and sexual harassment at work. What can people do in reaction if they find themselves in this really frustrating situation?

Let's start right off the bat by saying that if you are ever assaulted at work, sexually or otherwise, there is a criminal component to that, so in my experience, you want to call the police right away. Do that first and then worry about any civil or workplace or human resources issues later. Assault, sexual assault, and sexual harassment are all illegal, but assault is criminal.

When it comes to sexual harassment, in my opinion, you want to report it. And by that I mean that you take the time you need to feel comfortable with that idea, but you need to be aware that even though this is an issue for the civil courts, there is a statute of limitations, and in many states that limit is two years. So, if you're seeking compensation or legal redress, be aware of your state's laws and limitations and work around that timeline. I cannot stress this enough: Write everything down. Tell friends. Create a trail that investigators can work with to corroborate your accounts if you're seeking justice.

It hurts me as a human being when I speak to a client who has what I call "great facts"—what I mean by that is, really sad facts, really traumatic facts, facts that this person needs to live with for the rest of his or her life. But if this person never told her employer, never told friends, never told family, there is so little that we can work with as attorneys to create a path to justice because there is so little corroboration.

If this is happening to you, write your experiences down, keep a log of every occurrence, and consider telling friends and family who will be there for you if you decide to report this to your workplace or take this to a civil court.

Got it. So, let's say you can't endure a specific behavior any longer, and you do want to move forward with a report. How can a person go about that?

For a case to go as smoothly as possible, in my experience, you should report the behavior to your employer before you pursue any type of civil litigation. If you pursue litigation before reporting to your workplace, the discovery and deposition process can get dicey, and you will face a lot of questions about why you didn't go to your company first.

With sexual assault reporting of any kind, there's going to be police involvement. And what I say to my clients (those facing ha-

rassment or assault) who are not ready to come forward is to take
a lot of notes. That's really important. Talk to friends, talk to loved
ones. Those conversations can help you later. This all comes down
to: How do you build a sexual harassment case? Keep in mind that
there is probably not going to be physical evidence. So, the building blocks of corroboration and reporting and note-taking need to
be there.

One note on notes: Do not write them down at work! I've had
cases where a workplace deletes emails, you get fired, you get laid
off, you need to turn in your laptop, and suddenly your notes are
missing. Take your notes on your experience at home, on paper or
on a computer that you know you'll have access to for a long time.
Beyond the legal helpfulness of notes, taking these notes, writing
down your thoughts, and thinking through what happened can
also help with the healing process.

*Do you have any advice on when to tell HR versus when not to tell
HR? What's a workable timeline and a solid plan of action?*
You know, I'm so glad you brought that up. To protect yourself,
work from the assumption that HR is not there to be your friend,
they're there to protect the company they work for. In my experience, many clients have come to me surprised that HR was not
fully supportive of them when they reported their claims.

So, my advice would be to write everything down. And you
want to rewrite it. You want to read it. And that might take you a
few days, and that's OK, because getting this right is important,
and it's not a speed contest. If you've been harassed for several
months, and you decide that, for you, the path forward is making
a report, it certainly makes sense after you make that decision
to take a week to gather your notes and your recollections. In my
opinion, only then do you go to HR—don't walk in empty-handed.

Don't be afraid to sleep on this. Put the writing away, think about it, and go back a few days later when maybe you feel more confident. Go in to HR feeling strong and having your notes.

Another critical piece for the HR puzzle: Check your company's policy handbook. Many companies haven't changed their policies in decades—and that's important, because the company as a whole might not be following the rules they actually have in place. If you can walk in with your notes and with the company guidelines in hand, able to point out where actions are against policy, you could be in a stronger position to see the changes you want.

You don't have to say much. If you're happy with your notes and your account on paper, you should feel free to hand it in to them. That can work, especially if you are nervous and prone to being a people-pleaser.

That sounds so difficult. On top of your day-to-day work, which is hard enough, now you need to deal with this?

Sexual harassment or bullying of any kind in the workplace is really difficult. One of the challenges is that many times the predators will groom you into thinking you're friends, or even just friendly. Then something happens. And you question, "Wait, we're friends, we're close. Did what happened really just happen?" The person on the receiving end gets confused. These people tend to know what they're doing—often they employ behaviors that could be viewed with the benefit of the doubt. It's all part of their grooming process, so that they can continue their behavior. In so many cases, strong women are downplaying this. Because they're strong, because the comment or action doesn't destroy them or make them cry, they endure it and try to get through the day. They don't stop to think, "Wow, that was actually sexual harassment."

So ultimately, what can happen if you do make a report?
This is not for the weak. If you're seeing an attorney, you should
be at a point where you've thought about this, you've taken notes,
you've talked to multiple people in your life about this. Tough,
tough cookies come forward. I've noticed that very bright, organized clients will have lots of notes on what happened to them.
If they're coming to see me or any civil attorney, they've thought
about this for a long, long time, while being mindful of their
state's statute of limitations.

So it's commendable. As an attorney, when I pursue a restraining order or when I make a closing argument, I will often com-
mend my clients for having the courage to bring this out into the
open because this is not easy. It's really scary.

*Let's say you're still in the I-want-to-work-this-out-at-work
place. You're not yet contemplating involving an attorney.
Are there any specific buzz phrases when you make your case
to HR that will raise the probability of their following through
on your behalf?*
First, create a goal for your situation. Do you want to move to
another department? Change shifts? Have HR talk to the person
harassing you? Do you want to stay in your exact role and just
have the person simply not talk to you? Know all that before
you go in to HR and be prepared to tell HR what you want—
voicing that makes it more likely that your desired outcome will
actually happen.

Then, I bring the strategy back to the company's policy handbook.
Look through it for specific phrases that, in your experience, are
not being fulfilled by the company or by specific employees. Apply
the company's own buzz phrases to your story.

The bottom line is that you should go in with this mindset: I have a detailed story of what happened, I'm going to tell it to you, and I'm going to tell you the outcome that I want.

This is a civil rights issue—you have the right to work in a safe, respectful environment.

After graduating from Seton Hall University School of Law, Jessica Ramirez served as a law clerk for the Honorable Paul J. Vichness, J.S.C., in Newark, New Jersey. From immigration matters and family law to criminal and municipal cases, Jessica brings a wealth of experience to her practice at D'Arcy Johnson Day, where she focuses on sexual harassment, accident, and personal injury cases, work injuries, medical malpractice, nursing home neglect, product liability, defective drugs, and criminal law. Fluent in Spanish as well as English, Jessica is a member of the New Jersey Bar Association, the Hispanic National Bar Association, and the New Jersey Hispanic Bar Association. She has been practicing law for twenty years.

STREET SMARTS: VIOLENT ATTACK AT WORK

WORKPLACE VIOLENCE has tragically become such a possibility in American employment that the Department of Homeland Security has weighed in. In the event of an attack at work, specifically an active shooter, they advise:

▶ **Best, option: RUN.**
If there's an accessible path, try to evacuate the room or area. Don't waste time grabbing any belongings. As you leave, yell to others not to enter the room or area where the active shooter is present, and keep your hands visible so that any responding law enforcement agents do not confuse you with the shooter.

▶ **Second-best option: HIDE.**
Think of an area that's both out of the shooter's view and cover from bullets, and get there as quickly and as unobtrusively as you can.

If that means a separate room, attempt to both lock and blockade the door with furniture.

In this modern age, this can tragically escape our minds: Silence your cellphone! If your locked room has a TV or a radio, turn them off.

▶ **Third-best option: FIGHTING BACK AS A LAST RESORT.**
Fight back only if your life is in imminent danger. That can mean yelling, throwing things at the shooter, or improvising weapons.

CHAPTER FIVE

Security in Cyberspace

The Final Frontier . . . for the High-Tech Criminal

ET'S FACE IT—from banking to signing up for doctors' appointments, we're all doing more and more online. And all that activity just means more birthdays, more social security numbers, more addresses, more credit card numbers, and even more photos matching YOUR face to all of these facts . . . and it's all floating around in cyberspace. Your home and your car might be as secure as can be, but more and more I see people telling strangers online (yes, your recent online grocery purchase counts!) exactly where they live and their full name. But I don't bring a holier-than-thou attitude to the table . . . unlike some experts, who will tell you never to reveal this info, I realize that online life is the new normal—and we're never going back. So, sit tight—you need this chapter.

STANTON STORY

CHALK THIS STORY UP TO the shoemaker having holes in his shoes. Now, before I tell you this story, it's important to note that hubris almost got the better of me in this instance. One day, I was working on my computer, and it totally froze up. (A common occurrence, I know.) But unlike a usual freezing, I was immediately panic-stricken, because at the exact moment my computer conked out, a pop-up appeared on the screen: Call this number. So not being the most tech-savvy, and in fear that my expensive new computer was somehow going to implode, I did what every super-semi-famous security expert or naive octogenarian would do: I called the number on my screen.

Who picked up? A foreigner with a thick English accent, clearly from a place far, far away. What did he say? He needed immediate access to my computer in order to fix it. And how would he gain that access? I needed to push a series of keys on the keyboard and give them my password. Before I knew it, they had access. Relief! My computer would soon be back to normal.

Nope. Why did a CIA-trained security expert do this? What I just did was equivalent to letting robbers rummage through my home as I happily stepped outside my door. But was I acting in good faith? Yes. It takes superhuman strength, intuition, and yes, even the proper training (like you'll find in this chapter) to avoid the pitfalls of internet security. Take a look at these figures and decide for yourself:

BUT FIRST, YOU NEED TO KNOW . . .

A NEW PEW RESEARCH STUDY shows that even though Americans don't trust large institutions to keep their personal data safe, those same skeptics don't apply these same standards to themselves. What does that mean? They don't trust, for example, a credit card company to keep their data private—but skeptical Americans are also prone to handing over that same data. (See "Stanton Story" on the previous page . . . hey, I can laugh at myself now that it's over!)

From that same think tank, here's the very latest data on the breaches everyday Americans experience more and more often:

- ▶ Four in ten got billed for a fraudulent credit card purchase.
- ▶ Thirty-five percent got a notice that their personal information was compromised.
- ▶ One in five had their email in-box hacked.
- ▶ Fifteen percent were notified that their Social Security number was in danger.
- ▶ Fourteen percent had a line of credit or a loan fraudulently taken out in their name.
- ▶ Social media accounts were hacked for 13 percent.
- ▶ Plus, perception is everything. What Americans now think could be driving the current anxiety around all things online: About half of U.S. adults think their personal info is less secure online than it was just five years ago.

As a result, nearly seven in ten Americans have opted out of creating as many online accounts as they'd like, for fear of their information being used against them.

Passwords are the key to it all, right? Well, the vast majority of Americans keep track of their passwords by memorizing them or writing them down. That's a big problem—not because a dastardly thief is going to steal the piece of paper—but because that can point to you not creating new, unique, hard-to-guess passwords often enough. And yes, there are safe, online services that can randomly and confidentially provide you with new password ideas—and store them in the equivalent of an online safe.

That piece of paper is a big security don't for a separate reason—it leads to peace of mind . . . every security expert's nightmare, since it leads to complacency. Research shows that far too few Americans are worried enough about their password security. How do we know this? The amount of folks who have been hacked far outnumber the people who say they're anxious about password protection.

How likely is it that your identity isn't secure?

If you've purchased items online using personal information, we know there's a strong chance you're under threat. We know that nationally, identity theft and fraud hit an all-time high in 2017, with nearly seventeen million U.S. victims. Javelin Strategy and Research offers a yearly report on identity fraud, and found some really troubling firsts in their 2017 report:

Nearly a third of those surveyed were notified of an identity breach during the previous year.

You need to know that in a complete turnaround from years past, Social Security numbers are now being compromised more than credit card numbers!

What are the most common internet scams?

At the top of the lists compiled by major tech outlets right now: PHISHING. That means using emails or chats that look and feel legitimate, that lead you to a site that looks legitimate—but it's not, and if you look really closely, you'll see minor differences—anything that looks not-quite-real should be a huge red flag. Either the act of clicking a link sent to you in communication or the information you type in leads to bad guys obtaining your personal information.

Phishing became a major news story in 2016. Do you remember when Hillary Clinton's campaign chairman, John Podesta, had his personal emails uploaded to WikiLeaks? All that happened because he clicked a password reset link he thought was from Gmail, but was actually a phishing scam. As a result, bad actors learned his password and uploaded his emails for the whole world to see.

Another common culprit? Pay-me-or-else scams. Imagine opening an email that says: "You're grandson has been kidnapped—wire money to this account and we'll let him go," or, "I am an anonymous hitman, and you're my next target. In order to make it worth my while to not attack you, I need a check for this amount." This terrifying experience is unfolding as we speak, but it's a fraud. If you receive an email like this, contact the police and ask them to track down the sender.

Perhaps more common are the more subtle payment scams. Like phishing, these look legitimate, and it can be tempting to comply because the amount of money requested will be relatively small. For example, you might get an email from a company pretending to be Amazon, and they say your last payment of about $20 didn't actually go through—could you pay again? Well, if you decide this looks legitimate and pay, a criminal now has your credit card information.

Now, back to our story.

After several minutes of this far-away, foreign tech-wizard putting the fear of the Computer Gods in me, and telling me all the scary things that would definitely happen if I didn't follow their instructions, they told me that yes, my computer would be back to normal soon . . . if I paid a nominal fee.

Now all I needed to do was get out my credit cards and give them the numbers. I rushed to my wallet, seeking to get my computer functioning again as soon as humanly possible.

But then, my inner voice hit me with the blunt force of a stick, square in the head.

That stick = Jim Stickley. I had worked with him years ago at

NBC's *Today* show on cyberhacking and cybersecurity. Putting the good helper across the seas on hold (who was so eager to get the remaining number on my credit card), I immediately dialed a good friend who happened to be a cybersecurity expert. Luckily, he answered on the second ring, and after a quick run-down of what had just happened, he told me to right now turn off my computer, disengage the Wi-Fi, and hang up the other line.

As I've come to learn, this is a systemic problem faced by those with home desktops. The way these cybercriminals operate is that when you google Facebook, and spell it incorrectly, your IP address goes straight to them. They can then send you a virus, and they make it look like you're being notified by a trustworthy source— total subterfuge to the unsuspecting victim at the keyboard. The moral of the story? Know enough to know what you don't know and listen to your gut. When in doubt, or if you have any inkling that something could be "off," don't wait to be hit by a scam or a drained bank account to get on the right path.

And now, without further ado, cybersecurity expert, Robert Strang.

EXPERT INTERVIEW
Robert Strang

MR. STRANG BEGAN HIS LAW ENFORCEMENT CAREER in 1979 with the FBI in Washington, D.C. In December 1980, he graduated from the Department of Justice's Special Agent Basic Training class. From 1980 to 1989, Mr. Strang was a Special Agent with the Drug Enforcement Administration. There, he distinguished himself on numerous occasions, winning four major U.S. Department of Justice awards and two letters of commendation from the U.S. Attorney's Office.

***What's the best way to keep your identity safe and your
assets safe online?***

You have to keep on yourself and keep that willpower, even though
it's a chore, to do that basic thing we're all told about: constantly
change your passwords. Be careful of insecure locations when you
connect with Wi-Fi (for example, at an airport) and never use or
enter your personal passwords or information on that public domain Wi-Fi. It's really about keeping that willpower and sticking
to the basics—resist the urge to sign into your email on airport
Wi-Fi. Have that calendar reminder to change your key passwords. It's a chore, but it can save you time, energy, and money if
someone's coming after you online.

If there's any doubt at all about where an email or prompt came
from, don't answer it and don't respond. Phishing is a big problem, and that's one of the ways that most people get into corporations' systems—by assessing that it only takes one person in an
email blast to fifty thousand company employees to respond to
a request that looks like their bank, or looks like a company ven-
dor, or it looks official, and suddenly with just one username and
password entered, a hacker has access to the whole corporate
online system. That's true on the personal side as well—you just
have to be certain that you always initiate your interactions with
key contacts (like a bank or your email provider), and that you
change your passwords and commit, as hard as it is, to not using
Wi-Fi in hyper-public locations.

I've found in my years of experience that what's true for companies is also true for individuals. And you have to remember that,
as we sit here today in 2018, almost every government agency is
being or has been hacked one way or the other. We've seen this in
the Department of Defense, the White House, and certainly in
the 2016 Clinton presidential campaign, and so on and on it goes.

You know, at the end of the day there's really nothing that is totally secure that's out on the internet. If you wanted total cybersecurity, you would need to remove the internet from your life altogether— that would look like a computer in a locked safe that has no access to any type of outside or internet connection. We know that's not realistic. And if that's not realistic, we need to accept that everyone's assets are vulnerable when the internet is involved. You can even take money out of the equation—we know that simply information about people—be it addresses or credit card numbers— bring huge premiums on the black market.

Think about that. For example, my information is available out there because I worked for the government for ten years and in that timeframe some federal agencies were hacked. All of that background (sometimes personal) information was taken. So where is that information now? You know, it's probably in the same place that criminals on the black market can buy the information that people had stolen from using their credit card at Target, during the hack that made national news in December 2013.

It's not a pretty picture, but that's the reality we open ourselves up to when we use the internet.

Robert Strang serves as CEO of the Investigative Management Group, having honed his extensive government experience in fraud detection and prosecution into a unique investigative resource for the private sector. As CEO of Investigative Management Group, he is one of the world's leading corporate investigative and security specialists serving major financial institutions, Fortune 500 companies, large law firms, and high-net-worth individuals and families.

STREET SMARTS: DON'T STORE INFO ONLINE

Don't think you have a big online, digital, or internet presence? Think again. No Facebook or Twitter, you say? Get smart. Are you one of the . . .

▸ Thirty-nine percent of Americans who have a standing account with any company where they've paid a bill?

▸ Fifty-five percent of Americans who have an online bank account?

▸ Thirty-six percent who have an online account for their home utility bills?

▸ Thirty-two percent who have an online account at their doctors' offices, let alone their health insurance payments?

So, how do you keep your data safe when you've definitely provided your address, phone number, credit card number, and even health information online at some point in your life? Change these passwords and usernames as often as you can. Creating a bimonthly alarm on your smartphone is an efficient, no-stress prompt for switching them up.

Never save your credit card info with an online store. As tempting as it is (hey, who doesn't love a fast checkout?), nothing is worth the stress of proving to the card company that you didn't buy that new car the morning after the latest department store hack.

NINJA TIPS FOR SOCIAL MEDIA PLATFORMS

I've said it before, but this bears repeating: These different platforms need strong, long, different passwords that are changed frequently. Don't give bad actors, or hackers' algorithms, the opportunity to guess your password and use it against you.

Facebook

Facebook dominated the headlines in the wake of the 2016 election, not because of personal data breaches by bad actors, but because Facebook itself shared user information data and research companies, via one professor who had permission to use data from hundreds of thousands of users who consented to a questionnaire. If the United States Congress can't quite unpack whether this is legal or not, I certainly can't—but what I do know is that the way this data was used was against Facebook's policy, and that data sharing resulting in unintended consequences for the original user is rampant today. You can only control what you're aware of—so how on Facebook do you learn what you can control and adjust your settings and your actions accordingly?

> ▶ **Get serious.** Your life and your privacy are a big deal, and Facebook and bad actors are not playing around. Bad actors, or even those who simply want to spread your freely given information around, are relying on your being lax about all this. My recommendation? Set aside thirty minutes in the next few days, go to your Privacy Settings, and comb through what you can change to make your profile information both more private and less comprehensive.

> ▶ **Be wary, and selective, of the in-site "apps" you activate.** Activating these means you could be sharing whatever you're sharing with Facebook with that app as well. But here's the problem—once that app gets your data, they're not governed by Facebook's policies. They could be selling and sharing your information. In my opinion? The fewer apps on Facebook, the better. A 2018 report from the *Los Angeles Times* notes that if you delete an app on Facebook and want it to stop storing your information, "you need to reach out to the app directly to ask its developer to delete the data you have already handed over."

The first step there is checking which Facebook apps have your information. Luckily, Facebook lets you see this with apps you have not yet deleted. By clicking "Settings" and then going to the apps settings, you can see which are active. I recommend deleting any you don't frequently use—then, of course, getting in contact with the app's developers to demand that they delete your information.

► **Don't be afraid to leave fields blank, or straight-up fib.** High school you attended? Wife's name? Kids' names? Birthday? Full name? Email address? Just two of those fields truthfully filled in could let a bad actor triangulate almost all of your personal data and blackmail you, or worse. None of these answers is required to open and maintain a Facebook page. So ask yourself why you feel compelled to tell strangers you don't know—or your best friends, who, hey, know all of that information already—identifying information. Head to your Facebook setting right now, and delete or lock (so that only you can see the information) identifying data.

► **Think twice about using API: "Application Programming Interface."** Have you ever seen a totally different company prompt you with phrasing like, "Create a profile or login with Facebook." Hey, logging in with Facebook is easier—you don't need to create separate usernames and passwords, and your whole online experience can feel more user-friendly. But much like apps, you've now just opened up a new company to your personal information. For companies you trust and use often, that could be palatable to you. The Facebook security process is all about awareness. Ask yourself: Do I know which companies have access to my Facebook data via API? If the answer is no, check your settings and disable communication with companies to the greatest extent you're comfortable with.

IF YOU DO DEACTIVATE . . .

What's the difference? "Deactivating" is like pressing pause—your friends can't see your profile and you don't appear to be on the site, but you retain the option to "reactivate" at any time. With deactivating, posts you've made on friends' walls will stay up, but your name will no longer be "clickable" to your profile, which is now hidden from site users. Users also won't be able to search for you.

Any messages you've sent will still be visible, but now, you won't be able to send or receive messages. You can remain deactivated for however long you want, and you can reactivate at any time.

According to Facebook, "deleting" is more permanent. You cannot regain access to a profile that once existed, but no longer does, by typing in your username and password. Facebook says deletion is delayed for a few days, so if you change your mind and sign back in, you can reverse your decision. The entire process of deleting "data stored in backup systems" about you, says Facebook, can take up to ninety days. Friends will still have access to messages you've sent that they have not deleted. Facebook notes that copies of some material about you might remain in their database, but that they're "disassociated from personal identifiers."

Twitter

Consider turning location sharing off for your tweets. Letting the world know where you are with every tweet lets people know when you're home and when you're not. It could also facilitate stalking. To turn this feature off the next time you write a tweet, swipe the location indicator at the bottom of the tweet box into the "off" position—now, all future tweets will open with location "off" as the default.

Research your privacy settings and choose what works best for your security. Either the whole entire world can read your tweets, or only those who follow you can—that's the difference between a public and private Twitter account. You can also use privacy settings to make sure that no one can search for your account, and then request to follow you, by searching for your email address or phone number.

If you do want a private account, don't be afraid to stringently curate your followers. Never met the person? Sketchy-looking profile? Don't hesitate to deny their request to follow you.

Did you know that, like Facebook, Twitter also offers "apps"? Given the data sharing and communication that could be taking place between the companies, consider deleting any apps you've allowed and making sure you're comfortable with the terms and conditions of the apps you're currently using.

As always, keep personal info to an absolute minimum. Kids' names? Town? Alma mater? As we've discussed, these are all data that can lead to identity theft.

Photo-sharing Platforms

- **Less info is more.** As with all of these apps, don't feel compelled to fill in every field they offer, or to fib. Full name? Phone number? Stop people-pleasing, or as the case may be here, stop your compulsion to *app-please.* No photo service needs to know your phone number and your full name.

- **Go small.** In my opinion, all of your activity should be private—meaning that not just anyone who signs in to the account can see your photos. Lock your account, and approve your followers before they can start viewing your photos.

- **Turn off location-tagging.** Just like Facebook and Twitter, there are security risks associated with geolocating your photos. Do we really need to know exactly where this photo was taken? Probably not. If you really want to let people in on what you're enjoying, turn off the geo-tagging, but describe what you're seeing in the caption. Example? "Beautiful California sunset." Revealing an entire region is more vague, and likely more secure, than, say, an exact street in San Diego.

LinkedIn

LinkedIn is a fascinating security case study, because unlike the platforms we've already gone over, some degree of truthfulness is needed for the site's purpose—career networking—to come to fruition. Since LinkedIn is not the place to fib, ruthless protection of identifying information and ruthless standards when it comes to whom you'll connect with are key to keeping you safe.

▸ **Don't accept connections from people you don't know.** Well, let's soften that. You're new at your job, you're trying to network, and you've heard great things about a guy named Joe Smith in another division. You know he exists, you've seen him walking around, and his profile matches a person you know to be real. Connect, but proceed with caution. LinkedIn is a career tool, so if you're connecting with people outside your fields of interests, people you've never met, people whom you're not sure are real or not, that's definitely a security risk, but connecting with these accounts could also be a career risk, because you're literally connecting yourself to people you can't vouch for. We know that today in cybersecurity, phishing is a huge problem. On LinkedIn, phishing is present and works by connecting you to fake accounts that look real, and prompting you to reveal personal information. Don't fall for it. A great way to never have the opportunity to fall for that is to never connect with people you can't vouch for.

▸ **Use mutual connections as a barometer.** This person claims to work at your company, yet you have just one or two mutual connections? Sounds like a scam—don't accept this connection request.

▸ **Search your own name.** Make sure hackers or someone out to get you hasn't developed a page for you without your consent. If you do see pages or posts that are suspicious, you should report these to LinkedIn immediately by clicking over to their Help Center.

▸ **Keep private info private.** Despite the truthful nature of LinkedIn, security and privacy options exist to allow only LinkedIn to see certain identifying fields, but not others. Consider keeping your age and email address private, and leaving your phone number off the site altogether. Vague identifiers are best. Think college, but not graduation year. Think company I worked at, but not for how long. Remember, the compulsion to app-please is very real and these companies know we are itching to fill out fields fully and truthfully. Resist the urge, and your security risks could decrease.

BAD GUY POV FROM ROBERT STRANG: THE HACKERS WHO ARE OUT TO GET YOU

IS INTERNET SECURITY getting better or getting worse?

We're getting better all the time. But at the same time, so are the Russians, so are the Iranians, so are the Chinese, and so are the criminals all around the world. So we're all getting better—that's the problem. This space is evolving on the good guys' and the criminals' sides. They're getting better at what they do—so American individuals, companies, and corporations need to be constantly getting better at what they're doing. And like I said, sometimes it's as simple as sitting down at your computer for an hour and changing your bank, email, and 401(k) passwords.

Right now, the Chinese are looking for a lot of our business secrets. They're interested in how we're making things and what trademarks and patents we have—our secret sauces across industries. Several countries with bad actors want to stay a step ahead of us all the time. In particular, the Iranian government is looking at our government agencies. They're looking more at some of our government contractors. The Russians could be looking for information that they can use to help rebuild the Soviet Union. Every government and individual has a different motive for wanting to intrude on our system. But at the end of the day, whether it's consumer information from you and me or it's government secrets, everyone needs to be aware that there's enough organized technical ability in all of those areas to retrieve that information.

The more difficult you make it for the criminal, the easier it is for those criminals to give up on you and head to the next person. It's the sad reality that's true from a corporation's standpoint to an individual's standpoint. You can't stop the criminals, but you can make it more difficult for them.

CHAPTER SIX

Traveling Safely

Prep for the Unique Hazards of Being Away from Home

WHETHER YOU'RE YOUNG and impetuous, parents with children in tow, or approaching AARP membership, travel is generally viewed with equal parts dread and excitement. But no matter what, the destination you're heading to is filled with anticipation, so as a traveler, you often aren't paying as much attention to your surroundings as you should be.

Not too long ago, in the era of my grandparents, and even during the 1960s and '70s, travel was common, yes, but then again, it wasn't. For instance, my family didn't own "luggage." On the rare occasions that we traveled, we borrowed suitcases from family and friends. They were old Samsonites, certainly without wheels—and this is back in the day when everyone dressed for travel the same way they dressed for church. Folks smoked on planes, and applauded upon landing . . . boy, have times changed. Not only in the way folks dress (that's for another person's book!) but far more importantly, how the bad guys view today's travelers, and that travelers and vacationers are a constant target.

It was that mindset that prompted me to approach shows like NBC's *Today* and *Dateline*, ABC's *Good Morning America* and *Inside Edition*, and many other local and syndicated sites, with the idea that I would adopt the point of view of those bad guys and unleash on an unsuspecting public to see how'd they react—all on television.

Long before the infamous show *What Would You Do?*, there was yours truly. I vividly remember my senior producers Marc Victor and Noah Oppenheim at the *Today* show pitching now-famous segments where I'd tell viewers across the country that I'm going to "break into a 5-star hotel," "kidnap a kid in public," or "drug a girl in front of vacationers." The initial thought from the producer was invariably, "Yeah, sure . . . good luck with that."

Unfortunately, luck was totally unnecessary. We live among, and I hate to say it, a complacent public. People who I categorize as "sheep." Folks who follow the herd, even if said herd is running directly into the wolves. So, how to best defeat those wolves? Get real and think like one!

When I travel, I no longer think like a potential victim or survivor of an attack, be it personal or large-scale. Instead, I think like a king shepherd, which is a phenomenal dog that is protective, but not aggressive. (This breed just so happens to be the one I chose for myself, but more about that in chapter 13.) By that I mean that you can go about your travel and vacation being happy and excited, but also fully aware and ready to address any and all challenges that present themselves.

I've incorporated what I observed in my own king shepherd, Bishop, into my mindset. All too often, shooting those TV segments simply showcased widespread security vulnerabilities—this goes for travelers, but also the business that facilitate travel. (For example—why isn't your luggage scanned before you get on a train?) Airlines, hotels, casinos, and parks are made by humans, and therefore, they're not perfectly secure.

You've traveled by planes, trains, and automobiles a hundred times, or maybe even a thousand times. We're used to nothing happening when we travel, so when something happens, all too often, nothing happens by way of our reaction. That, my friends, can lead to a very bad day off.

STANTON STORY

HAVE VIVID MEMORIES of flying to visit my maternal grandparents in Puerto Rico as a child. It was a big thing back then to fly—so rare that my parents didn't even own luggage. I remember Mom and Dad making the calls to our extended older relatives who lived nearby asking to borrow some suitcases. It was a far more innocent time. Back then, family and friends could actually wait for you coming out of your plane at your arrival gate—an unthinkable concept today.

Since then times have changed. Americans travel now more than ever, and as travel has increased, unfortunately those bygone innocent days of travel look like they'll never come back.

Personally, I've had the opportunity to travel for many different reasons and by many means, from flying alongside Sly Stallone and a hundred of his closest friends for his sixtieth birthday, to

a no-frills prop plane with my beloved Lucy (a Teddy Bear Goldendoodle) for a speaking engagement, to old-fashioned click-
ity-clack trains from New York to Washington, D.C., for meetings.
Then, there are the typical cars and boats for work and play. What
remains constant in today's world, no matter how you travel, is the
exponentially greater chance for danger to strike than in the innocent days of waiting for friends at the arrival gates. And if you're
counting on the TSA to protect you? Don't! A Homeland Security
Agency test done a few years ago showed an abysmal 95 percent
failure rate—fake explosives and weapons on the good guys were
let through security in sixty-seven out of seventy cases by the TSA.

So what can a traveler do? First, don't let your smartphone turn
you into an idiot box. Situational awareness—and we'll teach you
how to gain that skill in this chapter—is your personal key to
safety and security. That theme is woven throughout the book—but
I would argue that it's most important when you're traveling, because ports of exit and entry in this country is where we tend to see
large-scale attacks. Get into the habit of scanning the crowd. Dress,
body language, actions ... Train yourself to PROTECT yourself
and loved ones. Don't dress for travel like you're spending a day
at the beach or nightclub—no flip-flops or high heels. Forgo tight
skinny jeans for travel clothes that have both form and function. I
personally wear either comfortable and secure sneakers or hiking
shoes, along with loose-fitting cargo pants.

Get into the habit of thinking about what law enforcement calls
"EDC"—Every Day Carry. For me, when I'm not traveling, that's my
firearm with spare mags, my CRKT K.I.S.S. pocketknife in matte
black as a money clip, a tactical flashlight, and, in my car, spare
flashlight batteries.

When traveling, modify your EDC items to local and federal compliance, and understand that the items you do take along could very well be critically important in a multitude of emergency situations. During 9/11, we know from survivor accounts that a flashlight made evacuation possible in several cases in pitch-black stairways when the planes' impact cut the buildings' electricity. And of course, a flashlight is legal in every state and airport.

While this may sound like a bit much for you—and you might not plan on traveling with a backpack of safety gear on your next plane, train, or automobile ride, remember that good habits are as hard to break as the bad ones.

BUT FIRST, YOU NEED TO KNOW . . .

Planes

The TSA finds about seventy firearms on carry-on bags every week. It is illegal to fly with your firearm near you (it must be in checked baggage), so it's safe to assume that an average of ten fellow air travelers in the United States any day you fly have bad intentions—or are comfortable flouting the law.

If your airplane crash-lands and passengers survive, the FAA estimates that you have two and a half minutes until even a small fire causes "flashover"—heat intense enough that the plane's seats and interior explode. That's why all commercial flights are designed to be evacuated in ninety seconds—a minute until flashover. Consider sitting close to those exit doors.

The FBI reported in 2018 that in-flight sexual assault reports are increasing at an alarming rate, rising 66 percent from 2014 to 2017.

Trains

The American Enterprise Institute has claimed that for the developed world, we have the least safe rail system—by far. *Fortune* reported that Amtrak's passengers get injured fifty-eight times as often as those traveling on France's trains.

Despite the harrowing, unlimited possibilities for terrorism on trains, baggage is not inspected in the United States before boarding, and neither are the passengers. Why? Some experts, like the first secretary of Homeland Security, Governor Tom Ridge, conclude that after 9/11, our government's laser focus went by and large to improving flight security, leaving trains behind—not only cross-state railways, but subways and commuter rails as well. In 2014, the Congressional Research Service wrote:

"Passenger rail systems—primarily subway systems—in the United States carry about five times as many passengers each day as do airlines, over many thousands of miles of track, serving stations that are designed primarily for easy access. The increased security efforts around air travel have led to concerns that terrorists may turn their attention to 'softer' targets, such as transit or passenger rail."

Automobiles

According to the World Health Organization (WHO), motor vehicle crashes are the number one cause of death for Americans when they travel outside the United States—so put those movie-based imaginings of kidnappings and food poisoning in foreign countries to rest.

Here at home, car accident deaths are increasing. In 2015, the latest year for which data is available, a staggering one hundred people died each day in automobile crashes in the United States.

What about unsuspecting bystanders? From 2014 to 2015, pedestrian deaths increased by 10 percent, putting the deaths of those on the sidelines at its highest number in two decades. Roughly fifteen Americans die this way each day on average.

You've probably heard the saying that you're more likely to die on the way to the airport than in a plane crash . . . that's absolutely correct, and it's never been more true. The U.S. Department of Transportation's research shows that the number of accidents and deaths in every single one of these categories is on the rise:

- SUVs
- Vans
- Sedans
- Pickup trucks
- Motorcycles
- Pedestrians
- Cyclists
- Alcohol-impaired driving

Hotels

Of all residential options, a hotel or motel room is the most likely to be burglarized. Yes, it's more likely that something of yours will be stolen from your hotel room when you're traveling than your home while you're away.

Here's what we'll address in this chapter, as well as a sample of the more detailed information you'll find here.

Traveling overseas, how to minimize risk but still have fun?
Do your homework long before you leave home. Save into your phone the country's national emergency phone number (their

"9-1-1") and consider sharing your itinerary with a trusted friend. For the region, town, or city you're visiting, look up local crime rates, weather, and any terrorist warnings or geopolitical conflicts that could escalate during your stay. No vacation is worth your life. Consider rescheduling if tensions—even if they're unrelated to your personal demographics—are boiling over.

What to do with jewelry while on vacation...
Hotel safe, or wearing your best pieces out and about? My takeaways in Ninja Tips might surprise you...

Who do you allow in your hotel room, and who has access?
Always use your peephole before opening the door, and always keep your door fully locked, even when you're inside your hotel room. Who has access? Virtually everyone who works at the place you're staying.

Who has access to your smartphone?
In the country you're visiting, does the government track digital traffic? Listen in on phone calls? In some countries, you can assume that the minute you touch down, civilian hackers are working to retrieve your banking and credit card information. Research your destination's cybersecurity holes before you leave, and based on what you find out, consider leaving your main smartphone at home and using a pay-as-you-go mobile phone during your trip. In these situations, share your new phone number with friends and family before you leave.

My checklist for what I think every purse, handbag, or pocket should have while traveling...

- [ ] Flashlight
- [ ] ID

☐ Pocketknife (but not in your carry-on luggage!)

☐ Personal alarm, like a whistle or a more high-tech gadget, an item that makes a loud noise in the event of an attack

☐ Phone charger. Your mobile phone is your first line of defense in reporting an emergency and letting friends and family know where you are—so make sure it's always working.

What you shouldn't have ruling your pocket on vacation: social media. Post the photos and thoughts when you get home to avoid broadcasting your location to bad actors, as well as making it public that you're not at home.

EXPERT INTERVIEW
Conan Bruce

CONAN BRUCE is a career security and intelligence professional with over twenty-eight years of service. He is a retired supervisory federal air marshal and a former police officer and narcotics investigator. Conan also served in the U.S. Army for twenty years on both on active duty and reserves. He began as an airborne infantryman, then served in civil affairs and PSYOP units as a senior noncommissioned officer with deployments to Bosnia, Kosovo, Haiti, and Central America. Conan received a direct commission after a tour in Iraq and finished his military career as a military intelligence officer. He has been featured as a security expert on the *Today* show, *Good Morning America*, CNN, and Fox News. After retirement from federal service, Conan served two years as CEO of Impavidus Security Group, providing corporate security to media clients and managing global development projects for government customers. Conan currently directs the Save The

Sheepdog Foundation, a nonprofit providing suicide prevention research and therapy to veterans, law enforcement, firefighters, and EMS.

Air marshals teach what they learn for aircraft safety to all transportation sectors—Conan actually traveled across the country to teach bus companies, and operators of cargo trains and passenger trains what he learned at the federal level.

Of his life's work, Conan says, "We took the philosophy of what we did and taught it to other people." Here are his thoughts on staying safe and secure while you travel:

If you're going to a subway station, an AMTRAK station, a bus depot, or an airport, for us, it's all the same. In that context, we refer to people getting up in the morning and getting somewhere as "public transportation." And the first thing that we like to tell people is that, when it comes to public transportation, you're far more likely to be the victim of criminal activity than terrorist activity. We see terrorist events on the news because they rise to the level of national news, but simple crimes occur far more often. Here's the good news in all that darkness: The precautionary measures for one are very similar to the precautionary measures for the other. If you're preparing yourself with safeguards to be ready (or as ready as you can be) for criminal activity, that roughly means that you're as ready as is possible to be ready for terrorism.

Most people tune out when they're traveling, whether it's a train, plane, or bus—and that's because in public spaces, people tend to feel that "somebody else" is responsible for their safety and security. And that's a reasonable thought—after all, that's why we pay taxes. The only problem with that is that it's not always true. Why? It's not possible that safeguards catch every single person in every space, every time. A lack of resources precludes 100 percent of people from being secure in any given public space. So if you believe that fact to be true, the logical reaction is taking responsibility for your own safety and security in public transit. Instead of tuning out, start by taking some responsibility, and then build on that.

In most public transit in the United States, you cannot be armed. That's not what I'm talking about, though it's a possibility there for you if you pursue legal and ethical avenues. So, how do you take responsibility for your body potentially experiencing a terrible crime, accident, or even terrorism without a concealed weapon? We call it "domain awareness." A lot of people say "situational awareness," but I like "domain" because we want to think of awareness as something total and 360-degree enveloping, as opposed to situational, which to me, implies a case-by-case basis—which is less helpful.

Arming yourself with the proper mental mindset is essential for domain awareness. If your brain is not engaged, you won't be able to travel with an air marshal's mindset. Jeff Cooper, a marine veteran and renowned security expert who passed away in 2006, developed the Cooper Color Code, and federal marshals expanded it to bring it into the mental mindsets that we see in modern public transit. The colors are white, yellow, orange, red, and black. White is total relaxation, total unawareness. We relate it to sitting on a couch and watching TV, but unfortunately, a lot of people bring this mindset to public transportation. Yellow is general awareness. You're relaxed and aware that you're traveling, but you're walking through your day aware that threats exist. We call this "relaxed yet alert." You're going through your day, and you're not so much switched on as you are paying attention. The next level is orange—we call this "heightened awareness." Something has gotten your attention. Whether it's a threat or not, you're able to process a situation and say, "Is this actually a threat to me?" Now, the problem with orange is that, while it's an intelligent and aware space, it's really difficult to maintain for long periods of time. It's mentally and physiologically exhausting because you're just a little more "heightened" than you are at any other time. You're focused and prepared, but this stage is draining. The next stage is red—which to us is essentially "fight or flight." This mental space is usually triggered by immediate danger. You need to act— whether it's fight, run, or freeze—and you will take one of those paths (there's no right answer), but red means that your mind is processing an action you'll take. You're not walking on by, choosing not to participate. With red, there is no way to opt out—the walls are falling down around you, versus seeing, for example, two people arguing across a room. Stage black is a wrong answer—and it's what we want people never to go to. Black is such complete and total mental and bodily panic that you might as well be blacked out. In "black," you're unable to think or act.

White

Unaware and unprepared. If attacked in Condition White, the only thing that may save you is the inadequacy or ineptitude of your attacker. When confronted, your reaction will probably be "Oh my God! This can't be happening to me."

Yellow

Relaxed alert. No specific threat situation. Your mindset is that "today could be the day I may have to defend myself." You are simply aware that the world is a potentially unfriendly place and that you are prepared to defend yourself, if necessary. You don't have to be armed in this state, but if you are armed, you should be in Condition Yellow. Aim to be in Yellow whenever you are in unfamiliar surroundings or among people you don't know.

Orange

Specific alert. Something is not quite right and has your attention. In Condition Orange, you set a mental trigger: "If that person does 'X,' I will need to stop them." Your pistol usually remains holstered in this state. Orange is a mental strain, but you should try to stay in it as long as you sense a threat. Once you realize you're safe, shift back to Condition Yellow.

Red

Condition Red is fight. Your mental trigger (established back in Condition Orange) has been tripped. The fight is on.

Normally, the general public walks around in "Mental Condition: White." When they're confronted with something that would trigger Red for people with domain awareness, someone in White goes straight to Black. What's ideal is to live your travel movements in Yellow or Orange, and we've found, with research backing us up, that when a threat comes to fruition, your mind goes to Red, not Black. Keep in mind that our research has found that Yellow is completely sustainable for the entire day. Orange is not—but can be sustained for short bursts. For example, air marshals are trained to stay at the beginning stages of Orange all day—which is exhausting, but possible with the incredible training we go through.

Again, the average person goes White to Black. Not only are these mental conditions not efficient or helpful, they're outright dangerous. Strive to travel in Yellow, and if you are living your travel life in Yellow, our research shows that a threat will trigger a Red mental condition. Now remember, Red is not perfect. Red does not mean that you make all the right decisions and survive 100 percent of the time. Red means you are able to react to an actual threat—whether that reaction path is flight or fight. Red means your brain will be capable of making decisions in response to your threat. Black means you're essentially blacked out. You can't make any decision, let alone a good decision. Now, maybe you do survive after your threat has triggered a mental condition Black. But if you do live, it would be survival by luck. Wouldn't you prefer to have more control over the situation, if at all possible?

This color coding may seem too touchy-feely, too academic, too elementary to you. That reaction makes sense, so let me tell you why air marshals—some of the toughest guys around—swear by it and teach it all across the country as opposed to just saying, "Well, get a concealed-carry firearm permit." We use this color code system as our first line of mental defense and domain awareness, and swear by it as the method that makes you as safe as possible based on decades of research, because when we travel internationally we often cannot carry firearms once we exit the aircraft. It's not like the movies, where U.S. agents can carry their guns wherever they please. In many European countries (and nations all across the globe), we are not permitted to carry weapons once we land, so we needed to devise a total mental and physical outlook for personal protection, and this is it. Often, we walk around as if we were civilians—the difference is, we've developed drills, teach them, and stick to them.

Everyone knows the line "If you see something, say something." I have another line that I think should be just as important to our national transportation conversation: Become a student of normal. How does someone order a drink at Starbucks? How does someone sit on the subway?

How does someone wait in line for TSA? If you train yourself for acute awareness of what "normal" is and what "normal" acts like, you'll be able to identify when something is off. So, look for normal—and what's dangerous will start to stick out more and more prominently as you use public transportation and its loading areas.

Anything is possible. "Possible" does not mean likely, but when the America we live in has a different harrowing attack story on the news every day, I want everyone to learn how to "travel in Yellow." So, I'm focusing on mental drills that arm you for scenarios you're likely to come up against.

Your number one takeaway should be taking mental notes on your surroundings and learning what's normal so that you can recognize what's abnormal. Number two is doing these mental drills, do possible scenarios—don't get too carried away with it, but just think through—"What would I do?" Mastering these two takeaways will make your travel inordinately safer.

If all you do is understand these color codes and understand mental readiness, and you take efforts to understand your domain, you have just increased your level of safety and security 1,000 percent, or by ten times. Plus, you'll be safer than the general public, which is, unfortunately (and I'm trying to change this), walking around in Condition White.

There are ways to dive deeper into taking control of your travel safety. Stay in tune with current events. Watch the news. Know what's going on in your city or your town, as well as anywhere you're going to visit. Look up a place on the web before you visit. (For example, has there been a string of recent robberies? It doesn't mean you're going to cancel your trip—it just means you're going to be walking around in Condition Yellow, not White.) Be as aware as you can. There is no value in getting wrapped up in conspiracy theories or paranoia, but research has shown that awareness of current events boosts an individual's safety and security immensely.

Now, you can merge mental drills and current events awareness. We all know that the most deadly shooting in modern American history took place in Las Vegas, Nevada, in October 2017. Run that mental drill. You're at a concert and gunshots ring out. What would you do? Where could you hide? Just entering any concert, let alone one in Las Vegas, you can bet Americans are going to be more aware. What's going on above me? Could an active shooter access a balcony or a high-rise nearby? Most people don't look up—why don't you start?

Air marshals and law enforcement officers are trained to always look up, down, 360 degrees around themselves by second nature. Again, I want you to travel like an air marshal—it all comes down to domain awareness. If something happens, we know what we're going to do. If you're in Yellow at a concert or a public event, knowing how far away you are from an exit, how far away you are from something that could protect you (be it from bullets, a fire, or simply other people—any kind of threat), just knowing where you would go and what you would do is going to save your life.

Why? Because you've already made the decisions. When you are presented with an emergency that pushes you into Condition Red when you've already been hanging out in Condition Yellow, you will not go to Black. Instead, you're engaged. What do I do? Do I get out of here? Do I fight back? You've already thought that through with mental drills, so you already know what you'll do or at the very least have an idea of what you'll do. And if you run those drills regularly, reacting effectively will become second nature.

One more topic to help keep you safe: target selection. Bad guys normally pick out their targets. Just acknowledging that is big, from a pickpocket to a terrorist. From specific to general, a victim is targeted for a reason. There are soft targets and there are hard targets, and you need to know that bad guys will normally take the path of least resistance—which is the soft target.

A hard target is something or someone that looks alert, some-one who's paying attention, someone who looks switched on. If it's a building, it may have armed guards or hardened structures around it. If it's a person, it may be a traveler with a briefcase tight in his hand, so that a bad guy can't just walk up and take it. Some-one who's paying attention. A soft target is a place or a person with a general air of complacency. You do not want to be tagged as hav-ing an air of complacency. Bad guys can spot that. They're looking for soft targets. We know that soft targets are the preferred targets of criminals and terrorists.

So, what we all need to do is work to become harder targets. I was in Bosnia during the Bosnia-Kosovo War, providing security for an ambassador. He would come out every morning to get into his car. But he didn't just get into it—he would walk around his car, kick the tires, look inside, obviously looking for anything "off." Criminals and terrorists surveilled him doing this every morn-ing—and observed that he was not high enough in the food chain for secret service to be at his house. Nevertheless, these criminals, we learned later, decided NOT to take out this diplomat because he appeared to be very aware and alert to his own security—a hard target. The criminals later explained to law enforcement that this is exactly why they did not go after him. You probably don't have secret service at your house either—but just looking like you're switched on could save your life. It can truly be that simple.

The easiest way to appear to be a hard target, research and expe-rience shows, is to stay in Condition Yellow. And we know that this follows whether you're in a tube that's thirty thousand feet in the air or four stories belowground.

Conan Bruce resides in Northern Virginia. He has raised four daughters, which has only added to his protective nature.

NINJA TIPS:
DON'T LET A VACATION RELAX YOUR SECURITY

Hotel Safety

YES, hotels often represent a luxurious break from our day-to-day lives (especially if we're using them on a hard-earned vacation), but statistics show you probably need to be more vigilant in hotels and motels than you do in your own home. Here are some strategic tips for staying safe:

Safe safe?

Be aware that hotel management or staff might have a universal key code to your room's safe. Yes, using the safe is better than leaving your wallet out on the bed, but it's not perfect.

Emergency calls.

If you're outside the United States, what's the national emergency phone number? Does that service offer English speakers? Most important, check before you leave that your cellphone will work properly where you're traveling, and that the rates work for your budget, so that you won't be tempted to turn it off or leave it in your hotel room. Murphy's Law says that's when you'll need it most!

Do not disturb—ever.

Turn-down service and room cleaning are part of what you pay for, but I recommend being in the room while it happens. Whenever you're not in your room, place your "Do Not Disturb" sign on your doorknob, so you know that if you're not in the room, no one is.

Get to know the neighborhood.

Where is the nearest police station? Fire department? And a question for some countries and regions: Is it safe to leave the hotel complex alone? Ask your hotel's front desk for their recommendation when it comes to a trustworthy, professional taxi service.

First floor? No thanks.

Try to avoid a room on the first floor of a hotel if you can. As with all structures, it's common knowledge that the first floor is the easiest floor to breach.

On that note, lock, lock, lock.

Even if you're in your room, keep your hotel door completely closed, engaging both the automatic door lock AND the typical swinging metal lock, as well as any chain or dead-bolt locks that may be on the door's interior.

Plan practice doesn't stop on vacation.

This is especially true if you're traveling with young ones. Before the fun begins, discuss escape routes and an emergency meeting place outside the hotel room while you're unpacking.

TV on.

Out and about for the day? Consider leaving your TV or radio on. An intruder (or even a dishonest staff member with key access) might think twice if they hear noise behind the door.

STREET SMARTS:
KEEP TRUSTED ALLIES IN THE LOOP

Copies for folks you trust. Heading abroad? Make photocopies or give photos of your passport, driver's license, and the credit cards you plan to take, and leave the copies in the United States with one or two people you trust completely. Consider doing the same with your general itinerary. ("Wednesday, I plan to visit the Taj Mahal.") In the event of a natural disaster or terrorist attack, your friends and family (and our government) will have the information they need to confirm that you're safe.

COP CRIB NOTES:
UBER, LYFT, AND RIDE-SHARING APPS

Getting into a car with someone you don't know is always a risk. That said, it's hard to turn down the convenience and ease these apps offer. In a perfect world, taxis would be a little more stylish and they'd meet you right at your door. As of 2015, taxi drivers are required to undergo a more rigorous background check than drivers for ride-sharing apps, and many taxis are subject to more stringent local government regulation. So, I have some very, very scant evidence that you might want to err toward taking a taxi. All that being said, police departments in major cities are not breaking down reported crimes to the level of whether they happened in a taxi or a vehicle summoned by an app. So, if you do use an app to hail a car, here are some commonsense safety and security tips:

▶ Before you enter the vehicle, make sure the name your driver gives you matches the name your app is showing. So don't say, "Is your name Joe?" (hey, they can just say yes!) Say, "Hi, what's your name?"

- Don't hesitate to use the app's own built-in security features. Many will have a "share" option, so you can show trusted family and friends not only exactly where you are, but also the driver's name and the car's license plate number.

- If you're unfamiliar with your destination, use a mapping app on your ride to make sure you're headed in the right direction. Alert your driver, or authorities, if you appear to be veering off course.

- Always sit in the backseat.

- Refrain from getting too personal with your driver and letting personal info slip. The apps do not share what these places mean to you—whether they're your work, your home, or your friend's house. Avoid saying things like, "Here we are, home!" "Another day at the office—thanks for the ride!" or "We're going to my daughter Mary's house—she lives at 32 School House Lane." Suddenly, they will be able to triangulate lots of information about you.

EXPERT INTERVIEW
Mike Keane

WHEN IT COMES TO TRAVEL SAFETY, in my experience, I've seen that people are focused on their travel rather than recognizing that they're out in a public setting. This is true not only in an airport but anywhere where there's a large group of people together, anywhere in a public setting. You need to be aware of your surroundings, and have not just your travel in mind, but also your safety in mind and your security in mind. That extends beyond just watching your bags and making sure someone doesn't take them.

The January 2017 Fort Lauderdale, Florida, airport shooting is a prime example of something that could unfortunately happen again. The shooter walked into the men's room with his bag, retrieved a firearm, came out, and started shooting people. If you're standing and just staring at the baggage carousel, waiting for your bag to show up, you may miss someone drawing a weapon behind you until you hear shots. It's a good idea to keep your head on a swivel. Keep looking around and look for suspicious activity, but also look for law enforcement entities so that you know where you can report to them, or where you can seek refuge with them if something happens.

The biggest thing that you can do to keep yourself safe and secure is to have situational awareness as to what's going on around you. Look for suspicious behavior, look for unusual things, and then report them accordingly, or in the dire case of an event happening, be able to react. For some people, that's running and seeking cover. For other people, it's hiding if you aren't able to run.

If you can't run and you can't hide, the response for some trained individuals, and the response for everyone (should they have no other option) is to fight back. Use whatever you can as a weapon. If you can't run and you can't hide, you must fight.

In the Air

Put simply, a vehicle or an airliner is moving so you can't leave. On top of that, there are very few places to hide that provide cover. Psychologically, we've seen that if one person gets up and responds, then more will follow. It was true on Flight 93. It's true in most circumstances: If someone reacts, if someone has the courage to do something, then many people will follow. It's amazing how many people are willing to help once the aggressor is down on the ground. The crowd mentality makes someone willing to grab an arm, willing to grab a leg—they're willing to help out.

There's an old saying that it's better to have an army of deer led by a lion, than an army of lions led by a deer. What it takes is someone to step up, someone to lead, and someone to have the courage to respond.

Idea: Auxiliary Air Marshal Service

The idea for better in-air security is that a person working in law enforcement—either active or recently retired, and proficient with firearms—volunteers themselves to be an air marshal on a flight, and therefore, they would be allowed to travel with their firearm in carry-on baggage (a notion that's currently illegal world-wide). Do you think that this is an idea that could possibly work or take hold?

If you relate this idea to what I said about fitness training and courage, and then you think about people in your own life that might be able to do this, I think it's an idea worth exploring. Immediately post-9/11, instructors from every walk of life, from elite military and law enforcement communities, helped out. These sometimes now-civilian individuals were very well trained, had strong situational awareness, and had the decision-making process already embedded in them. They were tactically sound, yet they were not allowed to carry weapons on an airplane.

Then I saw some air marshals come in through the academy who were having trouble lifting their own bag into the overhead compartment. And I thought, there's an injustice there. I mean, if an individual is willing to be tested, and has the training, and has the fitness level to pass a test that includes a physical fitness test and using the firearm, as well physically protecting the firearm, our society should think about taking advantage of that human resource.

This program would need to be a well-maintained, well-regulated, and well-administrated force. These talents are what we call a "force multiplier," and this might provide more coverage on planes. The program would have to be administered by a government entity. I believe that there are law enforcement teams out there that can administer and maintain a program of this nature.

Who do you see joining this program?
Just look at the active and retired Special Forces community, the retired law enforcement community—the number of people who could still pass the physical tests and the tests of the use and aim of a firearm. You could easily increase the coverage on aircraft tenfold. You could even have a philosophy that these on-plane forces only act in self-defense of terrorism, and outline strict limits to what prompts a person to engage. It's an innovative idea and it would have to be closely and well-maintained.

The elements of the program would have to be developed and strictly enforced because you can't just have anybody with a weapon responding to an active shooter or terrorist, because then you end up with a lot of collateral damage, a lot of rounds down range.

You need to have trained individuals who understand shot placement, understand knowing what's beyond your target, understand how to engage in a tactical arena. I don't think that it's something that the average firearm owner could do. But this could be worth exploring in the context of a trained tactical community.

OK, let's step out of the airports. How can someone travel securely in a train station, a bus stop, a port?
I think a lot of people are made aware of an event after the event has already started unfolding. Recognizing the precursors to an event, I think, are key and that helps the "See Something, Say Something" program. Helping that program is not just saying something when you see someone pulling out a gun. Perhaps you see someone doing what looks like conducting surveillance. You see someone counting their steps, timing their entries, and then you see someone who's watching a space intently. So situational awareness, I think, extends to simply recognizing people who could be up to no good.

Having the reporting structure is key. You need to know who you are able to call. I don't think a lot of people are familiar with the numbers that they can call or how they report some sort of suspicious activity.

Look, these bad actors are going to be in the malls, they're going to be on the roadways. These people are going to be in the bus stations and in the train stations. They're going to be in the subways. They're going to be at large gatherings. There's the opportunity here to accept the new normal and be willing to train and prepare for it.

The idea of innovative risk-taking is sometimes squashed, particularly in government and transportation, because you've heard them time and again say that they have to be right 100 percent of the time, and the terrorist only has to be right once. That zero-defect-ever mentality can sometimes stifle innovative thought. The idea that you are going to come up with something new also calls for the acceptance that it might fail. To mitigate risks, you develop programs based upon the experience that you have and what is already known. And that speaks to why you might notice that changes in security structure are slow-going.

Mr. Keane brings more than three decades of military and federal security enforcement experience to every tactical situation he analyzes. Keane is the former director of the Transportation Security Administration's Aviation Division. He served as the deputy federal security director of Washington's Dulles International Airport, as well as the lead instructor for United Airline's Federal Air Marshal Service Academy. Keane is a veteran Marine Corps officer, naval aviator, and F/A-18 pilot.

BAD GUY POV FROM CONAN BRUCE: RUNNING MENTAL DRILLS TO KEEP YOU IN CONDITION YELLOW

STAYING IN CONDITION YELLOW for optimum travel security isn't always easy, but there are mind games you can play to keep yourself there. Let's say you're on a bus, and you imagine, in your mind, that the bus driver loses control and begins plowing through parked cars. That may seem like a crazy thing to do as you're sitting peacefully on a bus, but a truly effective mental drill is to say, when totally fine, "OK, what would I do?" Would I leave or take my bags? Are my kids with me? What would I do with them or how would I reach them on this bus? Can I somehow open a window and leave the bus? These mental drills are key to understanding how you would react if something happens. This is exactly what visualization is—like what athletes do before they go out on the playing field. Baseball players going up to bat have mentally swung that bat millions of times. Physically, they've maybe swung the bat thousands of times—but mentally, they've done it millions of times. For traveling, you need the same mentality. Baseball players know what it looks like to have their ball go over the fence. You need to know what getting to safety looks like for you in an emergency.

You have to have already thought about this. What do I do if the airport just catches on fire? How do I get out of here? What am I going to do? What would I leave? What would I carry? Many Americans have this down pat for a fire in their home, but not a fire on an airplane or at a train station. What window am I going out of? Do I have a ladder? If you haven't run through these drills mentally (you don't have to physically do them—after all, how do you do a fire drill at an airport?), then you aren't fully prepared. Remember, when you're sitting there running these mental drills, nobody knows or needs to know what you're doing. But that is exactly what an air marshal is doing, and I want everyone to be traveling on public transportation like an air marshal. This is exactly what special ops servicemen and servicewomen do. We used to joke that you would walk by every car just waiting for it to explode. It might be a bad joke, but it's the truth. In our position, you've already thought extreme situations through.

These mental drills will save your life. You're on a subway and the subway stops. The conductor says the engine has broken down, and you'll be stuck underground for a few hours. But you know how to react because you've run through this mental drill before on your daily work commute.

CHAPTER SEVEN

Protecting & Preparing Children

It's Your Most Important Duty as a Parent

ORGET YOUR HOUSE, your car, your bank account... if you have children, THEY are your greatest asset, bar none. Without delving into every cliché in the book, your kids obviously take precedence over all else—as they should. One thing law enforcement officers and county jail prisoners agree on: Crimes against children are the most despicable acts committed. From school shootings by sick kids to sick adults seeking to trick your child into a car, danger lurks in the place we least expect it. No plan is foolproof, but the chapter you're now reading will enhance your know-how... and every little bit helps as we shepherd our kids through this rapidly changing world.

STANTON STORY

I WAS TWENTY-THREE YEARS OLD, single, and it was Saturday night. Should have been a great night, right?

For cops, working a nine-squad chart back in those days meant you worked rotating shifts: 8:00 a.m. to 4:00 p.m., 4:00 p.m. to 12:00 a.m., and midnight to 8:00 a.m. with rotating days off.

Translation: A free Saturday night for this young cop was a rare thing indeed, so not much could prevent me from hitting the nightlife with my brother officers . . . except for one thing: the home and family of Sergeant Al Parlato.

My mentor, Sergeant Parlato led the Eighth Squad in the Fortieth Precinct. You couldn't mistake Al as he boomed down the halls looking like Charles Bronson's twin. He laughed easily, but I never saw someone so serious and dedicated once the clock started.

I was honored when he approached me to be his police cruiser driver (the same car I'd drive the night my career ended). Soon after, he bought a small home with a first-floor rental unit—and you better believe I jumped at the chance to move in. I mean, I was still a kid at heart and didn't know anything, so living with Al, his wife, Donna, and their two kids, seven-year-old Chrissy and five-year-old Frankie, was a profound experience for me. They welcomed me and I felt like part of the family. So that night, free and clear for a whole Saturday, I could hit the clubs with the boys or . . . watch a movie with Al and the kids. A no-brainer.

At 9:30 that night, the kids' movie was wrapping up. Donna Parlato was pulling a restaurant shift a few miles away. Since she wouldn't be home for hours, Daddy the pushover let the kids stay up late. I walked in to hang out just as Al was making a hot dog for his boy after Frankie had seen a guy in the movie eating one.

I figured I'd win some brownie points as Uncle Bill with Mom away—we needed dessert. So I said hello and goodbye and jumped in the car to hit Carvel before it closed. While I was at Carvel picking out what I thought the kids would like best, the following happened:

In the kitchen, seven-year-old Chrissy screamed. Al had turned his back for just a second. He told me later that he knew it was bad, really bad, just by the sound of his daughter. Al turned and locked eyes with five-year-old Frankie. The kid still held what remained of the hot dog. But his face was scared and his mouth hung open. He choked out the words, "I can't breathe, Daddy."

Al knew it had to be the hot dog. A chunk got stuck down there. Al's a coolheaded guy and had all the training and experience of a thirty-year first-responder. He immediately started routine choking protocols—hitting the center of Frankie's back, then the Heimlich.

"Spit it out, Frankie," Al ordered.

"I'm trying, Daddy," Frankie replied. He could still speak, barely, but no air was getting in.

Now real fear hit Al. Everything he knew to do wasn't working. On every Heimlich push he expected to see a hunk of hot dog fly across the room from Frankie's mouth. It didn't happen.

Al jammed his fingers into Frankie's mouth to feel for the blockage. Nothing. He jammed his fingers down as far as he could, so much so that Frankie instinctively bit him. He couldn't feel any blockage. That was bad. That meant it was down deep, probably in the trachea. Frankie had lost some of his fight and started to turn blue.

Al picked up his son and took him next door to their neighbor, a nurse.

Now, there I am driving home, tapping the steering wheel to who knows what on the radio, with a Carvel ice cream cake warming up on the passenger seat, when I heard the first siren. Now, sirens in New York City wail pretty much 24/7. But this was different and my hackles were up. One vehicle after another whipped past me headed to whatever was going down. For that kind of response, I figured 1085-Forthwith, cop in distress. But then a bus (ambulance) flew past headed in the same direction I was. And another one. Now I'm thinking bad thoughts. Like, 1013, cop in desperate need of backup.

The memory of turning onto Brinsmade Avenue where we lived is burned into my brain forever. Flashing lights everywhere. First responders responding to … what? What was happening?

I parked down the block and sprinted to the house. And that's when I saw Al, my best friend, father figure, brother in spirit, mentor—the calm man in every storm—overcome by sheer panic and despair.

"It's Frankie, it's Frankie," was all he said.

EMTs rushed little Frankie out on a gurney to get him to the ER. Al jumped into the ambulance and it took off. Somehow in all of it, Donna had made it back and chased after the bus.

Later, in the emergency room, we learned that Frankie had passed away. The doctors said the bit of hot dog was lodged so deep in the boy's trachea that there was nothing Al—or anyone— could have done short of emergency field surgery to get it out.

This story, and this entire chapter, is written in love, honor, and reverence to Frank (our dear Frankie) Parlato. I thank his parents, Al and Donna, along with his siblings Eddie, Ally, Chrissy, Little

Donna, and Alexandria, for letting this heart-wrenching story be told. I wrote this book to prevent tragedies like this one from ever happening. Let's use every prevention we know and learn every proactive route we can take to protect the most valuable thing a person can ever have, a child.

Frankie's story is one of accidental tragedy. We can work to improve our safety know-how, fortify our environments, and take daily action to keep kids safe. But what about those who would intentionally harm children? Keep reading, because simply attempting to understand how bad things happen to our kids can prompt extra thought and awareness.

And that could save a life.

BUT FIRST, YOU NEED TO KNOW...

How many pedophiles and child abusers are reported and how many go unreported? How can you spot and prevent abuse?
The mistreatment of children is, unfortunately, on the rise. We don't quite know why, but the facts are staring us in the face. From 2012 to 2016, the number of children who received formal investigations into their circumstances jumped 10 percent to nearly 3.5 million responses.

Those are simply investigations—do these inquiries result in getting to the bottom of questions of abuse or neglect? It appears so, because we know that over the past four years, the number of known child victims has risen to 3 percent.

Of those victims, nearly 9 percent are sexually abused—meaning that solely from the cases that are called in and looked into, we know that more than sixty thousand American children are being sexually abused each year. Double that rate are being physically abused. What about the rest of the victims we happen to know about? They're being neglected.

Why is the suicide rate of children growing?

Among adolescents, suicide is currently the third-leading cause of death, and it's on the rise.

A look at the CDC's records of suicide rates by age tells us that a child under the age of thirteen takes his own life just about once every four days.

One study author on children's suicide says that while we still don't know for sure what's behind this alarming trend, an increase in bullying could be the culprit. Yes, bullying has been around as long as there have been humans, but now, with the advent of constantly available social media, bullying can literally follow a child anywhere they go with a phone in their pocket. The worst part? Parents often don't have access or even know about their children's online accounts.

How many children die from accidental choking each year?

Estimates suggest that on average, one child dies every five days from choking and that beyond that, twelve thousand kids are taken to the emergency room after choking annually.

But let's look at the top two causes of accidental deaths for each age group:

- **Ages 1–4:** Drowning, traffic accident
- **Ages 5–9:** Traffic accident, drowning
- **Ages 10–14:** Traffic accident (then suicide, then homicide by firearm), drowning
- **Ages 15–24:** Traffic accident, then unintentional poisoning (think drugs, alcohol)

What are the most common fatalities among children?
How can we prevent them?

From the day a child turns one until they're forty-five, if they die, it most likely will be from an accident. After forty-five, the leading cause of death is cancer.

From ages ten to thirty-five, the second leading cause of death is suicide.

That means that in caring for the average child, we need to be on the lookout for drowning and traffic accidents, and we need to be on the lookout for suicide—statistically, this is what's leading to death most often in our young ones.

For how to best avoid drowning accidents, check out our Home Pool Safety Checklist on page 89. For how to keep as safe as possible out on the road, see our Car Safety chapter on page 237.

STREET SMARTS:
IDENTIFYING SUICIDAL THOUGHTS IN KIDS AND TEENS

IN SO MANY YOUNG SUICIDE CASES that hit the headlines these days, the talk and bullying that led up to the fatal action, the ideation of the suicide, and sometimes even the final note or communication take place on a smartphone or social media. If you are a parent, do not hesitate to look through your children's accounts for warning signs—it could save their life. We discuss the security dangers of social media in chapter 5, "Security in Cyberspace," but there is a component of emotional danger lurking on these platforms as well.

For the most up-to-date information on suicide awareness and prevention, you can visit the American Foundation for Suicide

Prevention's website. They tell us that:

▸ "There's no single cause for suicide. Suicide most often occurs when stressors and health issues converge to create an experience of hopelessness and despair. Depression is the most common condition associated with suicide, and it is often undiagnosed or untreated."

▸ The AFSP's key warning signs include:

1. Talking about suicide, being a burden, or feeling trapped.
2. Increased use of drugs or alcohol.
3. Online searches for how to take one's life.
4. Visiting or calling people with more frequency (as if to say good-bye).
5. A stressful event, like rejection, financial troubles, or major transitions.

I cannot recommend enough that you continue to research the prevention of suicide—the headlines and national statistics suggest that rates will only increase as time goes on.

EXPERT INTERVIEW
Dr. Marisa Randazzo

Dr. Randazzo served for a decade with the U.S. Secret Service, finishing her service as the agency's chief research psychologist. Today, she's a managing partner of SIGMA Threat Management Associates. Dr. Randazzo is recognized as an international expert on threat assessment, threat targets, and threat prevention. Dr. Randazzo has trained more than 10,000 professionals in law enforcement, and when it comes to her second-to-none knowledge on violence in schools, it's worth noting that she co-directed the Safe School Initiative, an unprecedented federal report on school shootings by the Department of Education and the Secret Service. Dr. Randazzo earned her master's degree and Ph.D. in social psychology from Princeton University.

How do you talk to kids about making sure that they're safe without scaring or traumatizing them?
When it comes to safety awareness in kids, you want to focus on what kids can do, rather than the scary part of a potential emergency. If you think about how we were all taught how to do fire drills when we were kids, we didn't focus on the fire. We didn't focus on the bad thing, and what could happen. We focused on, "What can you do when you hear the bell?" When the fire alarm goes off, what do you do? And it's the same thing for teaching kids about all kinds of security issues. You don't want to focus so much on the bad stuff, which can be, obviously, very scary for kids. Kids' brains can't handle scary stuff, or traumatic stuff, the same way that adults' brains can. We really have to be careful about what we tell kids and at what age, but we can always focus on what they can do.

One great way to phrase this to your children is to say early and often, starting at any age, no matter how young, "If something scares you, tell me or another grown-up." So you can make it very simple from a young age. Additionally, early and often, you can say to your children, "If someone's doing something bad, whatever it is, tell me or a grown-up." So those are the two key phrases: If something scares you tell a grown-up, and, if someone's doing something bad, tell another grown-up. You're doing two things when you give your children that two-part message: You're teaching them to focus on behavior and also teaching them to focus on their feelings. If something feels scary to them, maybe it's actually completely safe and they don't know it yet, or maybe those feelings are pointing to something they should be cautious of and stay away from. Either way, you're helping them to learn to articulate that feeling. It's very simple: If you think "This doesn't feel right; this doesn't feel safe," then tell a grown-up. Repeat over and over to kids that they can ask a grown-up whether something is safe first, then decide what to do second.

A mistake that parents can make: We know there can be a huge focus in teaching kids safety tips on the concept of "stranger danger." In reality, kids are oftentimes at greater risk for being victimized or abused by someone they know, whether it's a family member, a neighbor, a coach, a youth minister, whatever it is—so if as a family you only focus on stranger danger, kids don't know what to do if it's someone they know. So again, as a parent, you want to focus on other people's behavior. If someone's asking you to do something that doesn't feel right or doesn't feel safe, tell another grown-up, like your parents.

Remind your kids that it's always OK to say no. You can say no politely, but it's always OK to say no. We inadvertently give kids a mixed message. Think about this common scenario: We're shopping at the grocery store and a friend of ours comes over. It's a common response to prod our child and say, "Say hello to Mrs. Smith; be polite, please! Say hello," but remember, that's a stranger to our child.

So what I try to do instead with teaching kids personal safety and security, from a very young age, is that I'd rather they be rude if they feel a situation is unsafe than default to saying hello to every stranger. I'd always rather my child be safe and thought of as rude.

As a parent, I'm cautious about making sure I'm not giving my own kids mixed messages!

We've all heard the horror stories of a victimizer saying to a child, "I lost my puppy. Can you help me find it?" Or, "I lost my cellphone and I really need to call someone. Can I use yours?" Essentially, a criminal makes a child feel like they have to help, and lures them into an extremely unsafe situation.

Adults should never need to ask children for help, and that's something you can tell your child repeatedly: "A grown-up should be asking another grown-up for help, not you." You could even say that yes, sometimes your parents, your babysitter, or your teacher might ask you to help with a task—and that's OK. But other than that, adults need to ask other adults for help when they're in trouble. And an adult you don't know should never ask you for help. Tell your kids that an adult can find help from another adult; they don't need to ask you.

So now with our kids, this is the point in the conversation where you say, "Let's focus on what you do do" if that scary situation arises. Say, "If an adult asks you for help, leave, and find another grown-up."

On that note of scary things happening, how often should adults practice safety drills with children?

I like to do them with kids a couple times a year. There are some great drills you can teach kids to make them "kidnap-proof"—or as kidnap-proof as is humanly possible. Once your kids are familiar with those types of drills, it's very effective to catch them by surprise. Make the drills a game, because the more you can make them fun, the less scary doing the drills actually is—and the more frequent the drills become, the more quickly in children you can actually create an automatic response to a bad situation.

The less kids think about the bad "what if" and the more they think about "If someone grabs you, what do you do?" the better. When you're teaching kids like this, you can really make it a game, because we spend so much time saying, "Use your indoor voice. Be polite. Behave. Don't roughhouse with your sister!" But when you do this drill, or play this game, and whenever it comes to teaching kids about safety issues, tell your kids: If someone tries to hurt you or if someone tries to grab you, "all our rules go out the window."

You get to be as loud, and as obnoxious, and throw the biggest
tantrum you can!

In cases like this, there have been examples of a child doing
exactly this, and the perpetrator just drops the kid and runs away,
because this was more than they bargained for. In the news, there
are stories of children who have done this in a Walmart or a car-
nival, for example, and whoever was trying to take them left the
scene quickly.

Kidnap-proof drill

Practice this with your kids, and make it a game after you
teach it to them the first time. Pretend to be the "bad guy."

Why is this fun for kids, and not scary? They'll love this drill in
no time, because they're allowed to scream as loud as they want
and fight as hard as they can!

Instead of using the word "kidnap" with your kids, keep it simple: Here's what they do if a bad person tries to grab them.

■ *Tell your kids, "Make yourself as heavy as possible. Drop to
the ground!"*

■ *Be as heavy as you can! Try to stay on the floor!*

■ *Yell, "You're not my mom! You're not my dad! I don't know
you!"*

■ *Yell, "Somebody call the police!"*

■ *Get your kids to be as loud and obnoxious as they can be!*

So, from a young age, you can teach kids drills like that and build
on them. The language around this drill shouldn't be, "We need to
teach you this because someone might grab you and take you away

from Mommy and Daddy forever, and if you don't learn this, we might not ever seen you again." Don't dwell on that—remember, present to kids the basics alone.

Instead say, "If someone you don't know tries to grab you; if someone you don't know says something like, 'Change into this dress—we're playing hide-and-seek from Mommy,' and it's someone you don't know, don't do it! And instead . . . " and then launch into your practice drill.

Encourage them to create a scene. Then, you can keep practicing and practicing. A friend of mine who was in the CIA frequently did this drill with his kids (they were moving to foreign countries all the time, and in crowded situations a lot) and he would just go for surprising them, and it truly became an automatic response in his kids. They'd drop, they'd scream—just remember beforehand to tell your kids to stop when you say, "Practice is over!"

Turning this conversation to adults—I know a lot of parents who just live their lives nervous. We live in a difficult world, and sad things happen, and I think it's really hard to raise kids these days. Do you have any advice on that?

Yes. When your children are younger than, say, nine or ten years old, think of parenting as the constant use of the same tactic put in place by Secret Service agents: You don't want someone you don't know to get between you and your kids (just like Secret Service agents want complete awareness of whoever's between them and their asset), whether that's physically at a crowded fair or mall, or even in the cyber domain. You don't want some other adult getting between you and your kids.

As they get older, it's all about teaching kids to take on those skills themselves. Encourage them to recognize, what's getting between me and my parents? Between me and my friends? Your child's or your teen's discomfort at an idea or a person should be brought to you as a red flag, without judgment from you. Stress to them that you're always there to listen.

For any parent who might feel overwhelmed at safety and security issues, focus on what you and your kids can do, and practice and talk about that, rather than getting bogged down by what you can't do or can't know.

What can I do? I can keep an eye on my kid. I can put a baby monitor near their crib so I can see them when they're sleeping. I can make sure I use a reputable babysitting service to run background checks on potential caretakers. I can make sure I'm never overwhelmed when I'm out at a busy place with my kids, or that short of that, I don't let being frazzled change my safety behavior. (One thing we've sadly seen in this field as a kidnapping strategy is that a parent, overwhelmed at, say, a checkout line or a mall, has forgotten something, and a stranger says, "I'll watch your kids. They're safe with me. Run and get your ketchup." We've seen criminals literally look for overwhelmed parents at big-box stores as potential victims.)

You can commit to never leaving your children with someone you don't know, no matter the inconvenience or for how little time you'd be gone—and the same goes for leaving kids alone, even for a few minutes, no matter how tempting accepting the (sometimes absolutely authentic and well-meaning) help can be.

Do what you can. As a parent, what you are always capable of doing is reducing the likelihood of you and your family being that opportunity for a criminal.

NINJA TIPS FROM DR. MARISA RANDAZZO: HOW TO TALK ABOUT TERRIFYING EVENTS IN THE NEWS—OR SCARY EVENTS AT HOME

Are there appropriate ways to explain a traumatic event to kids without scaring them, whether it be something in the news, or something they heard about at school, or even something at home—like seeing Grandpa suffer a heart attack?
If it's something in the news, as a parent, remember that you always have the option to not expose something to your child if you don't want to. One thing that I think is important for parents to know is that kids' brains aren't yet equipped to handle trauma the same way we see it, whether it's on the news or hearing something on the radio or listening to adults discuss something. So when you have children around, you may want to consider when you have TV news on, or when you have radio news on in the car. You may choose, and it may be helpful, to filter some of that out.

But let's not pretend that you as the parents are where their day starts and ends—we know children hear things you wouldn't necessarily choose for them to hear when they're at school, out running errands with you, or quite simply, they've grabbed the remote and are flipping through the channels. Let's say there's a traumatic event that's very nearly unavoidable for even the youngest minds: the annual remembrance of 9/11, for example, or a school shooting that a teacher or other students may be talking about. As a parent, I recommend that you take the initiative and have that discussion at home first.

Start a conversation by saying, "You may be hearing about _____ at school. Here's what I know [say a very, very basic sentence or two about the event] and you may have questions. Please know that I'm always here to answer your questions, and I would love to hear them, whenever you want. Feel free to ask me, or your teacher." And if schoolyard chatter beat you to the punch, be sure to ask what, exactly, they're hearing at school—that way you can correct what they know, without adding any details that are unnecessary for them to learn, depending on their age.

Before sending them off to school, an easy template uses loose language (without lying) that doesn't offer upsetting details, like this: "I heard something happened in a school in ____. I think some people were hurt, but I'm not sure exactly what happened. If you hear about it at school, can you let me know?"

Kids' brains physically are not yet equipped to process this type of information in the same way adults are. You shouldn't feel that you have to fully disclose every detail you know. If kids learn upsetting details before their brains are ready, research shows that learning that information can have a longer impact on a child's brain than that same info does on an adult's brain.

COP CRIB NOTES FROM PASTOR WAYNE FRANCIS: "A CONFLICT DELAYED IS A CONFLICT ESCALATED"

HERE'S ONE OF MY FAVORITE sayings when it comes to parenting: a conflict delayed is a conflict escalated. I think we tend to wait too long to make our relationships better. So by the time there's a big problem, you can admit to yourself that this was probably a problem you noticed as long as six months to a year ago. I always tell people, "in the absence of clarity, fill in the blanks." You should never give anybody the opportunity to fill in the blanks about you, your motives, or your opinions.

EXPERT INTERVIEW
Marilyn Chinitz, Esq.

MARILYN CHINITZ is a formidable advocate for her clients, guiding them through some of the most challenging transitions in their lives. She concentrates her practice in matrimonial law, particularly high-net-worth divorce actions. Marilyn is a skillful negotiator whose numerous high-profile and celebrity cases have received national and international attention. She has more than thirty-five years of experience in every facet of family law, including:

- complex divorce actions involving diverse transactional matters
- high-conflict custody cases
- international custody cases including the return of abducted children in proceedings filed under the Hague Convention
- premarital agreements and postnuptial agreements
- same-sex divorce/dissolution matters
- paternity cases

Known for her straightforward, creative, and responsive approach to representing her clients, Marilyn is as successful in litigation as in settlement negotiations. She has argued winning appeals in the appellate courts of New York, and in trials before the family court and the supreme courts of New York.

Tell us how family dysfunction affects that family's children.
The short answer is that many children are traumatized by their parents' arguing and sometimes subsequent divorce, and more people need to be aware of that if they are getting divorced or if they are arguing constantly with their spouse. I have a client with two children who found out in short order that not only are their

parents getting divorced, but their father has been having an affair. Once those kids found that out, they went on their father's computer and discovered that their father had not only been having an affair, but had been having multiple relationships for over a decade. When you're a child, your world falls apart when you learn that, and the devastation can manifest itself in different ways. One is anger, one is turning to drugs. Many high school–aged children now turn to smoking pot—which as a society we've accepted as relatively minor on the scale of any drugs they could be using, but the frightening aspect is that if it they get their hands on anything synthetic, they can end up dead.

Right.

So, you see how the parents' mistakes can utterly destroy these children. And I can see these kids really struggling. The challenge now is making sure that they don't spiral out of control.

And the possibility that they could spiral out of control is right in front of us. What happens is kids can either get very, very withdrawn, or they can get very angry, or they can become violent because they don't know how to express themselves properly, and they get very frustrated. So you have to be really very mindful of that, and prepare for it.

What the court tends to do is they appoint attorneys for these children while their parents are going through a divorce so that the children (not just the parents) have a forum where they can speak and express themselves—they can express their fear. What's great about this system is that not only do children get to fully and honestly release feelings of anger with someone who is not their parents. That attorney can also remind them that if they're engaging in bad behavior and they don't tell anyone, they're going to go deeper and deeper into despair. I strongly recommend that if you're going through a divorce, be open to your children talking on their own to therapists or an attorney. What can happen if they have no adults to talk to is really scary.

Let's say you're going through a divorce and you have three kids. How can you make sure they're staying on track?
Parents get so consumed with their divorce that they neglect the problems that their kids have with issues like anxiety or OCD. I see kids focused in on their own anger. During these times, so often the parents are just trying to keep the wheels on the bus that issues that a mom or dad with little to no stress would see, aren't noticed—like slightly slipping grades, slightly altered personality, or even a potentially happy update, like a high school guy asking someone out for their first date.

In very sad situations, I see two divorcing parents so focused on their hatred for each other that they neglect what their own kids are going through and what those children need.

If you are going through a divorce, try to keep a similar level of attention on your children as you did before you were going through it.
Exactly. And I see all too often that this doesn't happen. In some instances, you see the opposite of what I've described: The child really rises to the occasion, sees one parent or both parents falling apart, and, in a sense, becomes the parent. One young man I knew begged and begged his mother to stop drinking, and she tried but relapsed frequently, and the son began self-harming because it was the only way he could process his own frustration from an incredibly stressful situation.

So, kids are very much at risk and they're in terrible danger through the divorce. When parents are going through a dissolution of their marriage, so often, if they would stop and really take a look at what they're doing to their kids, those parents would make very different decisions throughout the process.

And it's truly children of all ages. I did a workshop many, many years ago—it was fascinating—with children ages five up until twenty years old, and the older kids expressed a very, very unique position. They said: I wish my parent or my parents were not trying to be my friend. I wish they set boundaries for me. Instead, they were so intent on making me want to align myself with them throughout the proceedings so that they could get custody, that they let me do things I shouldn't have done. In trying to please these older kids, parents going through a divorce almost allow their children to pick up destructive habits. That workshop was very sad for me.

Putting divorce to the side for a moment—let's say you're an adult who sees a child where you think something is wrong, but you're not that child's parent. What's the appropriate and efficient way to report a potential issue, and get it to stop?

Many adults actually have an obligation to report anything they suspect—every employed adult should check their local laws to see if they are what's called a "mandatory reporter" (like a pediatrician or many teachers.) Wonderful charitable organizations can also help you call and describe the situation, and they can lead you in the right direction on a very local, specific level. What we do know is that there are approximately two hundred reports or more every day of child abuse. The question is: How many are actually being investigated? And that's the real issue. Resources are so scarce for this issue—and results vary, of course, once an issue is being investigated—I've seen the guardians of children who are being abused let off the hook, and children who aren't being abused with charges leveled against their parents.

So the problem is that our whole system needs to be upgraded. It needs to be reevaluated and we need to get really, really good professionals who know what they're doing. But given all that, I can tell you this: As a regular person, as a citizen, it is unacceptable if you see a child who is in need of help and you do not help. I believe you are as guilty as the adult who is harming that child. How many cases are there where kids are being assaulted physically, abused sexually, abused emotionally, and people do not think it's their business to protect them? To me, that's criminal. Err on the side of caution, and you'll potentially save a life.

It's heartbreaking. It really is. I donate time. There are senior centers and I donate my time. Some elderly people are terribly neglected and it's very easy to spot signs of abuse if you spend time with them.

You've seen it all in your work. How do we stop the cycle of neglect we see all too often?

I really believe that the foundation of society is the family. A loving family not only needs to spend time with elderly family members but they have to be aware and proactive. So, the answer is vigilance. Be open to having your worst fears confirmed, and be open to looking more closely.

If you go into almost any hospital, you see how some workers handle elderly people. I mean, they throw their arms, they throw their legs, they push them into position. They don't feed them sometimes. And it's heartbreaking beyond words. That's why I think it's really important to donate time and volunteer. And you make a world of difference to that elderly person when you go visit a nursing home, because so often nobody visits them. And that to me is astonishing. There's an expression that I'm finding to be all too true in my work and volunteering: A mother can raise ten children, but ten children can't take care of one mother.

There's a lot of sickness in this world—and I think people have an ethical and moral obligation to stand up to anything that they see as being wrong and abusive. If you don't exercise that judgment call, it's my view that you are as guilty as the perpetrator. And if you can live with yourself after failing to speak up regarding a potentially abusive situation, that's pretty sad.

One time my daughter and I went shopping and we saw this mother repeatedly really smacking her kid in the face and pulling her hair. I went over to her and I said, "You need help. You can't touch that child again," and this mother started to mouth off to me. So I called over the security guard and I said, "You need to call the police," and explained the situation.

And here's the saddest part: I don't know what happened thereafter, but I do know that that little girl didn't even cry as she was being smacked, hard, right in the face. That tells me the child was used to being abused. Changing that child's life for the better is as easy as telling a store security guard that something's not right.

I'm always very mindful of how important the community is. You need to know who your neighbors are, you need to have a dialogue, and you need to have a chain of communication with your neighbors.

Bad things can happen and people can feel awkward, so they keep their mouths closed. And I'm not talking about gossip or chatter or anything like that—I'm talking about being vigilant and not being afraid to tell your neighbors about things you witnessed. "I saw Joey crying the other day. Do you think everything is OK?" Too many things in this day and age happen very, very quickly. If you feel that somebody is not right or something is not right, then you need to find out and investigate. Do your homework. Be observant.

When I say that, I mean that you can see if there have been any filings against a particular person. You can communicate with other people to see if they have the same instinct, or if they're aware of certain behavior that appears to be questionable. People need to be aware that they have an obligation to protect children and to protect other people, not bury their heads in the sand or look the other way. Whether we're talking about your personal life or your professional life, work with other trusted people to create a safety net for your community.

I think it's the obligation of every single person.

SPY SECRETS FROM MARILYN CHINITZ: DIVORCE PROCEEDINGS COULD "TAKE THE ROOF OFF OF YOUR HOME"

What else do parents need to know before they enter divorce proceedings?

When you go through a divorce, it's like the courts take the roof off of your house and they're able to look at everybody and everything. It's a very invasive process. Be prepared that your children might adjust to the situation by becoming manipulative, because they know what they can get away with when you're focused elsewhere. Be prepared to argue with your spouse about things you never expected to argue about. Be prepared to have the courts get involved in decisions like whether or not your child should be on ADHD or OCD medication after nearly failing out of school. Be prepared for your attorney or your children to reveal things about your spouse that you had no idea about.

Like what kinds of things?

It ranges from the mundane to the terrifying. In my worst cases, it's parents sexually abusing their children. They look so proper and they sound so intelligent and yet, they could molest children. One child of a client I represented ended up in a hospital during the divorce proceedings for a relatively minor injury, and it was uncovered by doctors at that point that her father had been sexually abusing her as well as her sister for years. And these were mid- to high-net-worth individuals, they had their lives together, and you would never suspect it. It's terrifying.

Of course, this sort of scenario is an outlier case when it comes to divorce proceedings. But like I said, in even the very best, most amicable divorce situations, you need to know that the roof is going to be metaphorically ripped off your house.

EXPERT INTERVIEW
Pastor Wayne Francis

WAYNE FRANCIS is the lead pastor of Authentic Church, a multi-site church in Westchester County, New York. In addition to his pastoral responsibilities, he serves in two community leadership roles for the Friends of the White Plains Youth Bureau and the PlayGroup Theater. He's married to his wife Claudene, who he always calls "Classy," and he has two teenage daughters.

How do we approach talking with our kids about difficult issues?
We're seeing a cultural trend right now where we're encouraged to be conflict-averse with kids. In contrast to that, it's my belief that parents need to normalize conflict, because working through conflict builds cohesion. I think people are less defensive when you

ask questions more often, because questions are normalized.

Kids tend to be open to answering questions that are not directed at their behavior but more directed to their thoughts. So I might ask my daughter, "Why do you like hanging out with that girl?" instead of "Why are you even hanging out with that girl?" I know that she might be influenced by a girl who I don't particularly care for, but I want to know what her driving motives are first. If I find out the motive, then I can better deal with the action. So be open to having an uncomfortable moment with your children. Take away the stigma in your own mind of actually bumping heads with your children.

Here's a key thing for me: Reward the behavior you want to see in teenagers. Recently, I did not want my daughter sleeping over at the house of one of her friends who vapes. So I didn't shy away from the conflict. I didn't let her sleep over, but I also didn't come down on this too hard with a reaction like, "Well, you can never spend time with this girl again." I said, "Talk to this girl, tell her that you're not allowed to sleep over at anybody's house this year, but that you are allowed to have people sleep over at your house. I'll buy the pizza, I'll take you shopping—I'll reward your taking control of the situation." So what some parents might initially see as a difficult conversation was normalized. Potential verbal conflict was normalized—and that just makes the next conversation easier to dive into. There's no need to say no to everything all the time. Set boundaries that you're comfortable with, and reward positive behavior.

Let's say maybe you haven't put the right boundaries in place, or maybe you have, and your child is acting dangerously. What can you do to help a child walking down a negative path?
Parents need to be very supportive. I don't believe anybody re-

turns to good behavior by control, they return through compassion. Boundaries and compassion can live in the same space: I will love you forever, but you cannot do drugs in this house.

You know you can obviously list the reasons why a behavior is wrong. If your children are making choices you taught them not to make, they're past the point of taking your lessons into consideration. We know that people need to feel needed and they need to feel known. If they've turned to drugs, it's possible that they don't feel needed and they don't feel known.

There is something broken in all of us that we're grasping after. The only way we reform our behavior is through compassion. There's no perfect parenting—you can do your absolute best and things can still go wrong. At some point, especially if your child is in his or her late teens or young adulthood, the only thing people can do is their best to love whoever they've been blessed to have in their life. We cannot control anybody, but we can control our output of love and compassion and being a listening ear.

Your conflict with your children can come from a place of compassion, because it's showing that you care. Again, normalize conflict early and often. Start these talks and disagreements and questions from a young age, so that they're anticipated by your children. You want them to think, "My parents are never going to stop loving me, but they do have standards and rules."

If you don't care about someone, you let them do whatever they want, you don't argue with them, you steer clear of them. Let's not treat our children like that. One of the worst expressions of love is to fail to challenge someone.

STANTON STORY

WHEN I WAS IN HIGH SCHOOL, "Lonely Boy" by Andrew Gold and "Lonesome Loser" by the Little River Band were big hits.

These songs reflected my own (and I'd guess many others') feelings of being alone and the inherent thoughts of real or perceived inadequacies of being a teenager in high school. But back then, I thought I was the only one.

High school memories are filled with firsts. First kiss, first heartbreak, first after-school job, first fistfight. Growing up in the Bronx, some of the aforementioned came sooner than expected—but what was never expected, and despite all the dangers, what never happened was a mentally tormented individual coming to my school with one or more firearms to exact their revenge for inner torment by killing as many people as possible.

While this current trend of devastating active shooters, especially in schools, has yet to be fully understood or even defined, in my opinion, solely going after the Second Amendment or blaming failures in "the system" to have not properly identified the shooter sooner are Band-Aid talking points. While there are valid points in many of these arguments, what we can actually do as individuals is learn from the past to identify the future. A lot has changed since my time in high school, even putting aside the music.

In order to approach any real impact, we must not rally around one specific issue, but instead work to prepare ourselves to confront an active shooter, hopefully before he (or she) starts firing.

In order to do this we must break down the possible motivations of potential shooters. Let's look at our culture. Back in my day, we passed notes and had a rotary phone, which we had to get permission to use to call a friend. Today's kids have social media and are sadly defined by their likes, retweets, followers, etc. For many, their social media presence is their whole identity, and their friends are all too quick to blur the line between the real world and what they see online. Just one cyber bully can have a profound effect on a young person's psychology. Properly reaching out to children and addressing any anxieties or hurt feelings is crucial.

On that note, schools and ancillary personnel must have a system where trained staff can identify, receive, process and SHARE information with one another and predesignated authorities. This way, a proper and in-depth analysis can be done by the group and fully informed decisions can be made—ranging from reaching out to the families of the student in question, to contacting authorities.

As we look back on past incidents, we're learning, and tragically, there are too many "what-ifs" and "should'a dones": having family members properly secure firearms, having schools following up with parents regarding high-stress students, and the list could go on and on.

Educating the educators, ancillary staff, parents, and law enforcement on how to understand, identify, coordinate, and address a potential school shooter is paramount. I count myself lucky that neither I nor the children I know, have experienced one. Soon, I hope this can be said by every single American.

Definition

An active shooter uses a firearm (or a few) to attempt to kill multiple people in a confined space—usually in a heavily populated area, often populated with people who the active shooter does not know. These situations are so often unpredictable, and they escalate and change at a moment's notice. What's tragic is that once an active shooting calms down—and in many cases, the shooter and countless others have died—the shooter's family, acquaintances, and colleagues come out of the woodwork to tell the media that they "had a feeling" this would happen. The likelihood that what I call a "pre-shooter" is in your life is exceptionally low, but if you suspect anything, you can call the FBI, explain your situation, and they will work to shield your identity.

School and Workplace Drills

Much has been made lately of the psychological effects of shooting drills on children. Nevertheless, many school districts feel that the work is absolutely essential. The National Association of School Psychologists has compiled a list of "best practices" for schools wishing to adopt regular active shooting drills, and I myself found them really helpful, since this sickening trend came about long after I was in grade school. The best-practice literature today contains experts' tensions between two models: the lockdown model and the "Run, Hide, Fight" model. If you're examining what would work best for your office or school, think about whether your team is realistically close to an exit and how you could all get quickly to that exit. In your space, are you close enough to the ground level that you can exit through a window? Or would it make more sense to shelter in the nearest metal bathroom stall?

One thing is for certain: In a school, trained, accredited psychologists and any school therapists should be apprised of every stage of the planning, so that they can offer recommendations, as well as tell teachers and staff ahead of time what signs to look for, after the drill, of a student who's been negatively affected or traumatized by the practice.

Pre-Attack Behaviors

Many active shootings don't make the national evening news, and don't come close to the number of fatalities of those that do. An active shooting can be as complicated as a mentally ill high school student shooting dozens of schoolmates, or as straightforward as a jealous partner whipping out a firearm in a restaurant and then being quickly tackled to the ground. Again: An active shooter is seeking to kill in a confined, populated space. In 2017, there were thirty active shootings across the country—and we could probably count on one hand those that were reported in the press.

The FBI tells us that to spot a person who might carry out an active shooting attack, skin color and background are poor indicators, as are illegal firearms, because a large majority of shooters appear to take pains to purchase their weapons legally. Active shooters are overwhelmingly male (94 percent), and yes, most are white. The FBI has also revealed that they can verify that roughly one in four shooters had a diagnosed mental disorder. We can surmise that a larger percentage likely had a disorder, but they went undiagnosed—because every single active shooter we know of displayed concerning, deeply troubling behavior before the attack. Active shooters typically spend (at minimum) a week planning the strike and have experienced more than three major stressors in their lives in the year prior to the attack.

Dr. Darrin Porcher
on Safety and Security at School

DR. PORCHER'S DISSERTATION IS TITLED "Reducing School Misdemeanor Assaults in Urban Settings Through School Collaboration Between School Leaders and Police." The purpose of this study was to identify how urban high schools can improve safety and reduce the number of misdemeanor assaults among students.

Dr. Porcher retired from the New York City Police Department as a lieutenant after twenty years of service. In his tenure as a member of the NYPD, Dr. Porcher performed a multitude of tasks. Dr. Porcher was assigned to the New York City Department of Personnel. While assigned to the Department of Personnel, he constructed the New York City Police Departments promotional exam for the rank of lieutenant. Additionally, Dr. Porcher was assigned to the New York City Police Academy in the rank of sergeant and provided instruction for over two thousand recruits during a three-year period. During the terrorist attacks on Manhattan in 2001, he was responsible for the supervision and rescue and recovery of victims in the World Trade Center complex. Additionally, Dr. Porcher was a lieutenant within the NYPD's Internal Affairs Bureau managing investigations of police corruption. Dr. Porcher also worked in the NYPD's Community Affairs Bureau as a manager tasked with the supervision and leadership of all police officers, detectives and sergeants within the City of New York.

Dr. Porcher is also a retired officer with the United States Army Reserve. As a commissioned officer in the Army during a time of war, he was tasked with ensuring that his unit was prepared in various aspects of counterterrorism. Dr. Porcher constructed a

series of homeland security and professional development semi-
nars for his military counterparts to ensure unit compliance. Dr.
Porcher is currently a professor of criminal justice at both Pace
University and Monroe College.

How can we keep our kids safe in schools, both physically and emotionally?

One of the things we look at on a national level is the propensity
for violence in schools. Looking back at the 1990s, we had the
Columbine attack, and in February of 2018 we had a similar attack
on a high school in Florida. You can see that we're facing the same
challenges in providing proper and adequate security for students
and staff. But by the same token, we say to ourselves that we don't
want to line the perimeter of a school with tanks, because our educational mission is that a school should be an environment that
induces learning. So how can we do it in an effective way?

One of the things that our educators must really focus on is
including their local law enforcement in the strategy to provide
security. It's my belief that ultimately the educator needs to be at
the forefront, meaning that the buck stops with the educator, be it
a university president or a local grade school's principal.

But how could an educator make shifts to a school's security landscape?

The law enforcement component should come in more as an
asset to provide a series of recommendations. We look at the
nuances in policing and enforcement changing so much recently, and the attacks that individuals want to attempt to make on
schools, and my own research suggests that the school administrators themselves need to be able to assess the pulse of not just
the students but also the connected neighborhoods.

Oftentimes you have issues where it begins as simply as two students having an issue outside of school, and the issue balloons and is brought into the classroom. With these cases, violence oftentimes spills into the school system, and the school administrators are unfamiliar with what's happening. So there needs to be a go between, meaning that schools shouldn't be afraid of maintaining constant communication with the police departments within their community.

Educators can then fortify your school accordingly.

How can a principal or teacher or professor learn what's going on in students' private lives, though?

The growing trend is that these disagreements and feelings—things that would have been inscrutable twenty years ago—are increasingly unfolding on social media. This has been coming to the forefront over school security over the last decade. These social media disagreements—or even bullying—absolutely could spill over into the classroom. So as a teacher, how do you find that out? You need to create a team that consists of educators, law enforcement, students, and someone with some street cred—someone who assists to bridge the distance between some of the educators and these kids' public social media habits. Don't be afraid to bring in some outside people who can give presentations to kids, who can provide them with their own testimony (maybe they had similar situations to your students) and how they themselves could have done better.

You need professionals who can guide that process, and I'm hoping schools can make the proper adjustments to their curriculum to really teach about flags for bullying or disturbing behavior.

The other side of these presentations and lessons is that we don't want the kids to feel ostracized after giving information to law enforcement or to school officials—though I think that kind of teasing or isolating is decreasing, given that many students realize that this type of information might stop an attack.

Your go-between person, your person with street cred (and hey, maybe it's just a cool teacher who gets along with students particularly well) can prove to be a tremendous asset in eliciting that information. This role is a key component in the assessment of what's happening on the outside and also the social constructs on what's happening inside the school. Kids typically don't want to talk about this stuff to police and educators—which is why a third-party entity, like a presenter, can be so helpful.

Most school security problems can be traced back to a disconnect among law enforcement, educators, and the student population.

If teachers are able to be more proactive on engaging situations as opposed to reactive, you're going to prevent a lot of problems. And it goes back to what I was telling you—you just can't line the perimeter of a school with tanks and think that will solve the problems.

I see things like metal detectors as more reactive than proactive, but of course both attitudes are important.

Why is a team of people with different areas of expertise perhaps more important than physical security measures?

At the largest high schools in the country, you can have upward of a thousand kids, and from a security perspective, maybe at maximum twenty armed security members on staff. That ratio isn't foolproof under an attack. I've found that proactive physical measures pale in comparison to proactive intelligence-gathering and community-building measures. Then you're working with the happy fact—yes, there is some happy stuff amid all this—that most kids want to go to school to learn. They're willing to work with you on creating a safe environment. Why not take advantage of that?

What happens if schools don't adjust mindsets?

If no one is willing to make that adjustment, we're going to continue to have instances like what happened in Columbine, Virginia Tech, and Stoneman Douglas.

My observation is that we're using rudimentary means to combat a problem that's both very complex and becoming more and more prevalent in our society. So far, not many people have stepped up and said, "Hey look, we need to add more mechanisms to this game." It just hasn't happened. And things don't seem to be getting better.

Ultimately you have a lot of sincere good; you have people who have good-natured thoughts in terms of combating these issues based on their negative experiences that have happened in the past. I think that goodness is a valuable resource that we need to start using in a big way.

Dr. Darrin Porcher received his BA in Organizational Management from St. Joseph's College, and an MPA from Marist College. In 2012, Dr. Porcher received his doctorate in Educational Leadership and Policy from Fordham University.

CHAPTER EIGHT

Countering Terrorism

Be Aware and Safe in Soft Target Areas

O F ALL THE CHAPTERS in *Prepared, Not Scared*, this one needs no introduction. Nearly daily on our TVs and our Twitters, we hear the harrowing, stomach-turning details of the latest attack on innocent people. When it comes to terrorism, so many Americans are cognizant of how much they don't know—and many times, they'd like to keep it that way . . . an understandable response to a weapon so unpredictable and so deadly that you might be tempted into blocking off your own education, right? Wrong. From attacks in NYC to attacks in the Middle East, we've seen that for those who do have a choice in the matter . . . the rare possibility to escape (and far too often, so many innocent lives do not have that chance) . . . education and training leads to safety-based decisions in the heat of the moment—no small feat. You owe it to yourself and your loved ones to keep reading.

STANTON STORY

EVERY DAY, FOR MILLIONS OF AMERICANS, it's the same controlled chaos: waking up, getting the kids ready for school, dressing for work. With the kids on their way, you jump on a bus or a train, or drive yourself to work. Traffic, crowds, and thousands of people, all rushing to punch that clock. Every morning: set and repeat, day in and day out. All the while, we're looking forward to the weekend and family fun.

The biggest problem with all this? Fighting through mundane routine and, simply put, the complacency it breeds. We know the morning rush was just as I've described on a clear September day when thousands lost their lives to terrorism in Manhattan, Pennsylvania, and the Pentagon. In the blink of an eye, that day became anything BUT routine. Tragically, there are evil forces at work inside and outside our society that want to change OUR paradigms. Of course, there are many different forms of evil: child abusers, gangs, murderers . . . but terrorists are a different and heinous breed unto itself. A quick Google search defines terrorism as "the unlawful use of violence and intimidation, especially against civilians, in the pursuit of political aims."

I'd like to add to that definition. It bears mentioning that a terrorist's radicalized ideology, whether it be for political or religious reasons, is primarily to murder the weakest, most vulnerable, and most innocent at the time of their attack, in order to maximize their agenda. This sheer unpredictability and innocent loss of life creates fear and dread, dissuading us from living our lives as we see fit.

The year 2001 was a long way back. Since then, America has endured isolated incidents of shootings, beheadings, and vehicles used as weapons. This type of terrorism is primarily sourced by radical Islamist extremists seeking to destroy all who don't think with their own demented view. Malls, movie theaters, schools, trains, planes, and automobiles—all places and things we routinely travel to, use, or enjoy—have now become the "soft targets" most desired by these cowardly terrorists.

This chapter will explore, explain, and provide examples of how you can harden the safety and security for yourself and loved ones in soft target arenas. Before we drill down into it, I ask you to do your own research and reconnaissance on your way to work.

Take mental notes and observe just how many people have their heads in the clouds. I'm not always talking about tourists looking up at skyscrapers—sometimes people with their heads in the iClouds are worse—and those are just the ones who are walking, using mass transit, and yes, even driving. Our culture and its creation of the so-called smartphone has collectively become individualized "bubble boys," noise-canceling headphones on, staring virtually hypnotized into our phones, cocooned from the rest of the world and focused on whatever it is we're looking at—but the terrorist predator just sees sheep, unaware, in a herd, and ready for the slaughter.

My goal is to make you "Prepared, Not Scared" and bring out your inner king shepherd! I make this analogy because (besides loving this particular breed of dog for multiple reasons) a king shepherd is always aware, protective, and ready, willing and able to take action if and when necessary—traits we can all use.

Walking around with a parachute? That's paranoid, not prepared.

If you work in dress clothes, consider toting around sneakers. Maybe even a seventy-hour bag filled with easily transportable cash, food, and bottled water.

Even though it's been quite a while since I've been in uniform, I'm constantly seeking knowledge and updating my own training. With some of the premiere operators in the field in the world, I train at Alliance Tactical Training Center and confer with ex-CIA and Special Forces experts on how to deal with the threat of terrorism around us. Do I expect everyone to train to that level? No. But there are fundamental, simple strategies to mitigate terror threats that won't save you every time guaranteed, but will maximize your safety and minimize your risk.

By the way, educating yourself to identify the threat and react accordingly by taking safe, secure, and tactical reactions can help everyone and anyone. No need to break out your inner *Die Hard* to help others and do the right thing. My motto? Do what you can to not make it easy for the bad guy to kill you.

BUT FIRST, YOU NEED TO KNOW . . .

- ▶ In developed countries, deaths from terrorism surged in 2015, rising by 650 percent. The majority of terror fatalities in the First World were the result of attacks in Turkey and France.
- ▶ Most people think ISIS and al-Qaeda when they think of terrorism, and we challenge you to shift that paradigm, which can leave you vulnerable when you least expect it. There are two hundred and seventy-four known and active terror organizations around the world.
- ▶ In the years since the 9/11 attacks, the worst year for terrorism was 2014, with 32,765 people murdered across the globe.

▶ OK, let's look at this with a more local lens: here at home, the one-hundred and fifty-six deaths from lone-wolf attacks over the last ten years represented 98 percent of terrorism fatalities in the United States.

▶ In the most recent year on record, ISIS carried out more than sixty-five attacks in First World countries alone.

▶ When the authors and experts of the Global Terrorism Index rank the deadliest countries, the United States is typically in the top quarter of that list.

▶ How many terrorist cells are estimated to be active in America? We don't know. But here's what we do know: Terrorism can seep out from any ideology, skin color, race, or religion. In 2017, Homeland Security Secretary John Kelly revealed that the FBI was conducting active terrorist investigations of cells in all fifty states.

▶ Change your mindset to build your awareness: Extremist domestic groups could be plotting more frequently than whatever paradigm you hold for what a terrorist looks like.

▶ Thwarted plots and terror-related incidents from right-wing extremists could be even more frequent than those from Islamist jihadists, new studies suggest.

▶ Commonly targeted groups by antigovernment or white-supremacist extremists (but I would call them terrorists if they're planning violence) include:

Federal, state, and local government employees. Before 9/11, the deadliest terror attack on U.S. soil was the Oklahoma City bombing of the Alfred P. Murrah Federal Building, apparently motivated by Timothy McVeigh's irrational hate for U.S. government.

Nonwhite individuals. The Anti-Defamation League notes that just after targeting government employees, the second-most-frequent motivation for right-wing terror is racial.

Individuals seeking to obtain or doctors providing abortions. Just under two dozen terror attacks were carried out with these targets from 1993 to 2017.

▶ Stop paying attention to the number of incidents, and start paying attention to where we're seeing the highest numbers of casualties!

Alex Nowrasteh, a terror expert at one of America's most prominent think tanks, writes:

"My terrorism research focuses on deaths committed by terrorists because that is the easiest and the least ambiguous metric to analyze the damage committed by terrorism. Attacks could be as minor as a pipe bomb left by a bulldozer that explodes at 2:30 a.m., or as deadly as the 9/11 attacks that killed 2,983 people and caused billions in property damage, so counting the number of attacks by ideology does not reveal much."

NINJA TIPS FROM CONAN BRUCE: LOOK FOR WHAT NORMAL LOOKS LIKE, BECAUSE NOT NORMAL COULD BE A BIG PROBLEM

LET'S SAY I'M SITTING ON THE TRAIN or the bus that goes from the parking lot at the airport to the airport terminal. Picture scenarios for the people around you, all with the backdrop of "What's normal?" What do people usually do when they're on this bus? We know that they're usually not talking to people (because they don't know them), they're usually on their phones, they're not making eye contact, exhibiting shallow breathing, possibly even pacing. Maybe they seem nervous. Maybe they're late for their flight. Maybe they don't like traveling. Maybe their spouse just yelled at them before they left because they forgot to do something.

We have no idea—but all of those behaviors are the same indicators as a bad guy right before he's getting ready to do something. But if you play these mind drills, and you know what normal looks like, you'll begin to be able to distinguish, well, "That could be what normal looks like at an airport" while noticing behavior that could either be simple preflight nerves or attack planning. Something you can repeat to yourself is, "Paying attention." As in—"That gal yelling into her phone is weird. She could be in a fight with her boyfriend. Well, I'm paying attention." If you see something not normal, say something. The worst that could happen is that you were wrong.

SPY SECRETS FROM DR. JOHN SPEARS: IT'S SAFE TO ASSUME YOUR COMMUNICATION IS BEING MONITORED

What do you think people need to know about terror attacks that might not be obvious, talked about, or intuitive to us?
We know that ISIS and al-Qaeda have documented their desire to attack us where they can create mass casualties—that's for the purpose of psychological as well as economic damage. So what comes to mind? Public venues. That's most likely sports events, concerts, open-air events, or mass transportation hubs. That's why, at these events, we see what could appear to be an extreme amount of physical and electronic security.

Without giving away specific tactics, techniques, and procedures, it is safe to say that you are being observed and your electronic transmissions are being monitored, all in an attempt to anticipate and help provide for a safe environment for the people in that environment.

That being said, if you are a citizen who's concerned with your safety, and if you're a responsibly armed citizen who thinks that being armed is an essential part of your responsibility to provide for you and your family's safety, the only guaranteed way to avoid a mass casualty incident is to never be in a large public venue. Your firearm will not be allowed inside.

Dr. John Spears

Tell us about your experience in the armed forces and as a doctor.
I'm a doctor of osteopathy, so as opposed to M.D. we go by D.O.
My background in the military was in the United States Army
Special Forces. I was an 18-Delta, which is Special Forces medi-
cal sergeant, and I served in the 7th Special Forces Group in the
Republic of Panama, and spent the 1980s doing counterinsurgen-
cy and counter-narcoterrorism in Central and South America.
From there I went to the 12th Special Forces Group Reserves and
finished college, and then subsequently went to medical school. I
then did an orthopedic surgery residency followed by a spine surgery fellowship and practice—so I'm an orthopedic spine surgeon.
So I have nearly thirty-five years of experience in the field.

In the late 1990s, with the global war on terror heating up, I
returned to consulting and teaching special operations forces. I
worked as an advanced tactical trainer for EAG Tactical, and am
currently one of the directors of Forge Tactical as a weapons and
tactics instructor.

*Wow, you have a long résumé. Let's say that a person is living
their normal, day-to-day life, and a terror attack happens.
What can a normal American do to help themselves and the people around them?*
The everyday response to trauma in the age of terrorism is where my
expertise lies, especially in a public venue. I know you've written in
this book about how to notice potential threats or react to an unfolding terror attack when you're traveling, so I'll just build on that with
specific reactions that can save your life and other people's lives.

You know, as a result of terrorism and terrorist-type tactics in the West, and now in the United States, we are seeing that the injuries resulting from these attacks more closely resemble war wounds—they're more the kind of injuries we typically see on the battlefield than traditionally the kinds of injuries that we see in the homeland from civilian kinds of trauma. Today, attacks involve tactics using the tools of war, like mass shootings, the use of vehicles to produce injuries, and the use of explosive devices to produce mass casualties.

Our first aid training and our reaction needs to catch up. These wounds are significantly different from the kind of trauma we've had to traditionally deal with in the homeland—I'm thinking motor vehicle collisions, unintentional injuries, stabbing wounds, single gunshot wounds from handguns—those kinds of non-war-fare trauma and how we respond to that with first aid is completely different from the wounds we're seeing become more and more commonplace as a result of the tools that people are using to commit acts of terrorism and produce mass casualties.

When considering their family's safety, the way somebody then may think about what knowledge they need and even potentially what kind of equipment they might need to deal with an attack has to be significantly different from what we all learned growing up.

The incidents that I think are the most relevant—in other words, what we need to learn to react to—within the West (certainly in the United States) are the 2013 Boston bombing and the Ariana Grande concert bombing in May 2017. It's only been fairly recently that we have started to see the person-borne IED used outside of the Middle East. The Manchester, England, bombing at the Ariana Grande concert utilized a suicide vest—and I believe was the first incident of a suicide vest used in the West. In my opinion, it's the hallmark incident of new terrorism in the West—

the new normal. So as a society, we really need to expand our horizons and start moving on from gym-class first aid.

The third incident that deeply concerned me—and pointed to a new normal—is the botched person-borne IED attempt at the Port Authority Bus Station in New York City in December 2017. Had it detonated, it would have been the first successful use of a person-borne IED in the United States.

So putting all of these things together, it would be irrational to ignore a trend for the use of these kinds of mass-casualty-producing weapons when we are considering the kind of threats that we need to prepare for as individuals.

We have to change the paradigm that we think about from traditional first aid. The kind of reaction that can deal successfully with these incidents and injuries falls under the doctrine of what we call tactical combat casualty care.

So, as opposed to thinking about motor vehicle collisions or unintentional injuries, we're now thinking about ballistic injuries from bullets, fragmentation from grenades and explosives, blast injuries, and injuries from overpressure.

So let's dive in.

We've identified that when it comes to preventable deaths, there are three classes of problems that go on to kill a person when their death could have been preventable. In the medical field, "preventable" means that if you identify the problem and you treat it correctly, you're most likely to save somebody's life. Massive head trauma, massive chest trauma, massive pelvis trauma—these are classified as non-preventable deaths—or at the very least, it will take a large team of individuals reacting immediately to save someone.

There are three major types of problems where we can intervene and we can prevent somebody from dying: massive bleeding, a

specific complication from a chest injury called tension pneumothorax (where air builds up in your chest cavity and that pressure
causes additional trauma), and airway obstruction.

Saving as many lives as possible on the battlefield meant teaching soldier how to identify and respond to a preventable death.
So we started training people in the military to get away from the
civilian paradigm of dealing with trauma, and we started training
soldiers in how to deal with actual, modifiable battlefield injuries.
So again—how to stop massive bleeding, tension pneumothorax,
or an airway obstruction in its tracks.

Let's look at those three incidents I mentioned again: the Boston
bombing, the Manchester suicide vest, and the attack that could
have been—the New York Port Authority bus station attempted
bombing.

Those kinds of devices and those tactics produce mass casualties where fragmentation from the device causes missile injuries,
primarily to people's extremities—to their arms and their legs.
The kind of thing that kills these people from those weapons is
simple: Major vessels, like arteries, are damaged and people bleed
to death.

Here's the answer we're using in the military: The immediate
response must be to apply a device called a tourniquet. Pretty commonsense kind of stuff, but like anything commonsense, it bears
repeating over and over again to help make things clear.

The rationale behind the absolute importance of the tourniquet
is that in the last fifteen years, the most indispensable item that
everybody in the military is required to carry at all times is the
tourniquet.

We have pushed very hard to get law enforcement in this country at all levels to accept that. We have worked very hard to destroy
outdated methods of thinking and teaching. It used to be thought

that tourniquets could cause more harm than good, because it
might damage the limb. I say, sure, that could happen, and that
person, whether they have an amputation or some nerve damage,
will at the very least be alive to thank you—so go ahead and use
that tourniquet.

*So what can we carry around every day, and what can we use
from everyday life to be prepared for injuries that result from
an attack?*

It is almost impossible to produce an improvised tourniquet that
is in any way effective, especially in the lower extremities. For sale
online there are many brands of what I would call professional-grade tourniquets that can be kept in your pocket or your
bag. The ones that are the most effective are those that have a
"windlass" mechanism, which is simply a kind of tightening bar
you can turn that can compress something as large and muscular
as a leg or an arm. Remember, the artery must be pressed shut so
that the blood stays in the body. A similar tourniquet is used in op-
erating rooms across the country whenever someone gets surgery.

But the kind of tourniquets that normal non-doctors and
non-military folks can carry mimic those used in the military—"Combat Application Tourniquets," or C-A-Ts. These are
small and made of nylon, Velcro, and fabric. If you're open to
carrying one, I'd ask you to be open to carrying even two or more.
They are small, discreet, and inexpensive.

If you don't carry a tourniquet, you absolutely should try to use
something you see around you. But I can't advocate for carrying a
C-A-T enough, because chances are, you will not be able to gener-
ate enough compression to stop an artery from carrying blood.
Plus, it's virtually impossible to apply any tourniquet to yourself if
it's not windlass.

Where on the body and when do you apply a tourniquet?

If heavy bleeding isn't stopped, the victim will eventually go into shock and die. We use tourniquets because we know that if you can keep the person's blood inside their body, going where it's supposed to go, they are going to be much better off.

Recognizing that somebody needs a tourniquet is also pretty straightforward. Let's start with the most obvious: If a person has had a limb amputated, there is no question that they need a tourniquet applied, because that's the only way to stop the bleeding.

Here's the rule of thumb: The tourniquet needs to be applied closer to the heart—usually that means higher than the level of the injury. In practical terms, the person who is at the point of wounding and first applies a tourniquet is the person who has the greatest chance to save the victim's life. It's my belief that everybody needs to be trained in how to use a tourniquet.

Let's take the 2017 Las Vegas shooting—an example of the type of attack where tourniquets and some basic emergency know-how might help.

People are in an open-air venue and are in the field of fire of a madman spraying them with bullets. If you can't get yourself to cover, you can't help somebody else. If somebody is injured in an open area, and you're trying to treat that person in the venue they were wounded, you're both liable to become further casualties. You can't stop and do perfect first aid at the site.

The first step is that you have to get that person behind cover. You have to get out of the area. Then and only then can you apply some kind of first aid.

The only treatment that you might render, right on the spot at the point of wounding, is to apply a tourniquet because you can do it extremely rapidly. In a situation like that, you may not be able to identify exactly where the bleeding is coming from, so we teach people to apply the tournaquet as high on the limb as possible. That means on your lower extremity, you're applying the tourniquet at the top of the thigh, up in the groin area. For an arm injury, you're applying that tourniquet as high on the arm as it will go—up into the armpit. Trust me, when pulsatile bleeding is occurring, the clothing will be soaked and you will not be able to see where the wound is. Turn the tourniquet until the bleeding completely stops.

Then you get out of there. You're getting help, you're getting behind cover, in safety, as rapidly as possible. If you are a victim of these horrific events, your thinking should be as simple as 1) Stop the bleeding. 2) Get to cover. Do whichever makes the most sense first, then do the second item.

Where can we learn more, absolutely factual information?

The Department of Defense has a website that reviews the principles of "T Triple C" (Tactical Combat Casualty Care). I'm pointing you here instead of to first aid sites because the injuries you see on a battlefield are the same ones you're likely to see in a terrorist attack that happens in your hometown. It's loaded with instructional and teaching material and videos that anybody can look at and learn from: https://deployedmedicine.com/. If somebody can't get live training from an instructor, Deployed Medicine is a second-best opportunity to learn. For somebody who has been trained, it's a fantastic way to go back and refresh yourself on how to do something correctly.

What other injuries can civilians on the ground help with when it comes to preventable death?

Sometimes, a massive chest injury can be treated on the spot. Just like a tourniquet can be bought inexpensively online, so too can an "occlusive chest seal"—basically a very effective, professional-grade dressing. This seal is another item that's easy to carry in a purse or leave around the house. These seals have a small hole or little hose in them to avoid potentially deadly "tension pneumothorax." Maybe you've seen this on TV—air builds up inside the body and can cause death.

If someone is unconscious, put them on their side, so that their vomit or their tongue doesn't plug their airway and cause a preventable death.

If you could choose only one item to carry with you that would most likely save somebody's life, what would it be?

There is no question that statistically the tourniquet would win as the number one item that a person should carry with them.

How can a person or family prep for their ultimate safety at say, a concert or a football game?

It's not revealing any classified tactic, technique, or procedure to say that those who are planning terrorist incidents prefer to have the event occur when the greatest number of people are present.

So therefore, before any major event, when people are gathering, or during intermissions or halftimes, is when people are most likely to be in large concentrations, either going to the bathroom or going to concession stands. There are areas within most of these venues where people naturally will congregate in large groups. You could decide with your family to plan on avoiding those large concourses and the places where people gather around vendors, especially during intermissions and at halftimes.

If you can plan your seating, you may not necessarily want to look for the best seats for a view. If you could plan and choose your seat, you might want to choose seating that puts you close to a major exit.

Remember, a tourniquet is not an offensive or defensive weapon. It is a lifesaving device. I'd encourage bringing a nylon and Velcro tourniquet with you, which goes without saying, because I think that if you own one, you should have it in your purse or your pocket as you go about your daily life. Plus, you can purchase concealable first aid kits meant for everyday carry.

You should also be able identify where the uniformed officers are if you see something and need to say something. There will also be non-uniformed officers within the venue. You need to be aware that the person coming to help you may very well be a plainclothes police officer

I don't think that the risk of terrorism should prevent Americans from going to public events. Every time that we decide not to do something, it creates a certain amount of psychological imprinting that we're supposed to be fearful and that we're not supposed to live our daily lives.

But certainly it's clear that terrorism, or at least the tactics of terrorism, are becoming more and more prevalent in the United States, as we have seen happen in Europe, and that a failure to prepare individually for that possibility could change your life.

BAD GUY POV: IF THERE'S SUCH A THING AS A TYPICAL TERRORIST, WHO IS IT?

INSTEAD OF PINPOINTING HOW to spot a typical terrorist, let's look at (and look out for) the typical terrorism we've seen unfold most frequently. Terrorism expert Max Abrahms has coined a term that describes these crazy, loner terrorists: the "loon wolf." Abrahms was early to the game, tweeting the term back in 2014—sadly, too many "loon wolf" attacks would still unfold.

West Point's Combating Terrorism Center's journal described the intersection of Islamic State–inspired terrorism and mental illness in January 2017. To my mind, anyone who commits crimes this devastating in such far-reaching ways is insane. But to the folks who study psychology, that's not always the takeaway. The authors of the West Point research point out that one study suggests that "lone-actor terrorists were thirteen and one half times more likely to have a mental disorder than group-based terrorists." Amazingly these rates are consistent with U.S.-based far-right ideological crimes—those who act on their own are far more likely to have a mental illness.

OK, so terrorists who act alone are a little loony. Thanks for the tip! Why is this notable?

Because online communities that are group-based either attract or outright recruit, literally seek out, mentally ill people to carry out the least enviable tasks. Seeking acceptance, they acquiesce to planted ideas or fully formed ideas from thousands of miles away. In that sense, their aims, while deranged, have some rationale. And that's what makes them trackable—if this were totally unpredictable, we wouldn't be able to stop lone wolves before they start.

What can we do? Israel has just claimed that monitoring social media has cut down significantly on lone-wolf attacks. So while we civilians can't monitor to the extent we might like, we can pay attention to what we're seeing on our feeds. If you recognize anyone expressing an intent of violence or fighting words toward others, consistent with the mental illness and mental instability so common in lone wolves, don't hesitate to tell the police.

CHAPTER NINE

Car Safety

Hot Wheels and Cold Steals

FOR MOST AMERICANS, besides your home, the most expensive thing you possess is your car. In recent years, our cars have become more and more like our homes: TVs inside, stereo systems that rival the best interior design options, and leather seats. It's only natural that we then treat our cars as an extension of the home—for many, this is where critical mistakes are made. We'll leave both valuable and sensitive items in our car, the same way we'd leave them on our kitchen table. I know this, you now know this, but the bad guys have always known this.

Think about what you leave in your car: mail, a computer, headphones, even our children.

Unlike a home, you should never, ever leave anything valuable in your car, even when it is fully secured. We've all heard the tragic tales of parents "running into the store for one minute" and then leaving their child in a running car.

There are ways to dramatically minimize anything happening to you, your property, or your vehicle in this chapter. You will get tips, statistics, and some commonsense wisdom to keep your car as safe and secure as possible.

STANTON STORY

'M ABOUT TWENTY-TWO YEARS OLD, and in my mind, I had the best car money could buy: a 1981 two-door Mustang with T-tops, black-on-black stick shift, and I looked great in it. One problem: It had four cylinders, and went zero to sixty in about fifteen seconds. Being young and a cop back then, I had a certain sense of invulnerability, which extended to my wheels. I was sadly enlightened of reality when I was about one hundred miles from home, on the New Jersey Turnpike, with a flat tire, trying to push my car on the highway. Had things gone any differently, you wouldn't be reading this book right now, because I wouldn't be around to write it.

If you were to look into the trunk of my Audi SQ5 hatchback SUV, you'd be lucky to fit a lunch box back there. The reason for the lack of space? I've tried to prepare for every contingency within imagination. (Check out "Cop Crib Notes" on page 248 for everything a smart, prepared car owner needs in their trunk.)

I am in a lane of traffic, not being prepared, not a tow truck company number in the car. What could have been a fairly easy and painless situation turned into my being nearly hit and killed by a tractor-trailer.

Always have either 1) a number and money to pay for someone else to move your car, or 2) the tools to do it yourself.

BUT FIRST, YOU NEED TO KNOW ...

What time do most fatalities occur because of drunk driving?

▶ If we break the day up into three-hour segments, by a long shot, fatal drunk driving accidents are most likely to occur between 12:00 a.m. and 3:00 a.m. After that, the next-worst segment is 9:00 p.m. to 12:00 a.m.

▶ Time of week is also notable, with nearly double the fatal alcohol-related crashes taking place over the weekend.

▶ In fatal, alcohol-related crashes, the driver is most likely to be twenty-one to twenty-four years old.

What are the most popular types of cars to be stolen?

Hold on to your Honda! Of the top ten cars models stolen in 2016, the most frequently taken two were the Accord and the Civic. Rounding out the list, in order ...

▶ Chevrolet Silverado

▶ Toyota Camry

▶ Ford F-150

▶ Nissan Altima

▶ Toyota Corolla

▶ Ford F-250

▶ Ford Econoline

▶ Chevrolet Impala

Where specifically are cars most stolen from? Home, office, or store parking lot?

▶ **Stats.** More than seven hundred sixty-five thousand cars are stolen in America every year, and 42 percent of those are never recovered. The average loss to the owner, all told, is nearly $8,000. Unfortunately, we are seeing car theft increasing.

▶ **Time of year.** Perhaps unsurprisingly, summer is the most common time of year to get your car stolen.

▶ **How often?** On average, a car, truck, or motorcycle is stolen every forty-one seconds in America.

How common are car accidents?

▶ **Accidents.** More than six million vehicular accidents occur each year in America—and those are just the ones called into police.

That means more than sixteen thousand four hundred accidents on your average day—or, an accident every five seconds.

▶ **Injuries?** 2.4 million people are injured in these more than six million crashes.

▶ **Fatalities.** On average, every day in America, more than one hundred people die in traffic accidents. For the latest data available, the fatality rate is increasing year over year.

1. Just under a quarter of those deaths are related to speeding. Just under a third are a result of alcohol-impaired driving.

2. For half of car-occupant deaths, the victim was not wearing a seat belt.

3. For 40 percent of motorcycle deaths, the rider was not wearing a helmet.

4. A troubling side note to all this is that in the midst of these collisions, pedestrian deaths are on the rise, increasing by 10 percent year over year for the latest available data set.

EXPERT INTERVIEW

Thomas Ruskin

How have cars changed over the last decade or so to make drivers safer?

When you get into your car in the morning, you might not even think about the features a car has now to keep you safe that it didn't a decade ago. Look at automatic locks: In most cars today, when you put them into drive, thirty seconds to a minute afterward, your doors automatically lock. This stops anyone from being able to, at a stoplight or otherwise, just come into a car. When

I was a kid, air-conditioning was an extra; now it's standard. Then there's the fantastic feature called OnStar, and many cars now that don't offer OnStar offer a similar emergency system. The health and comfort—and therefore driving abilities—of the people in the car are now seen as something necessary, not extra. So people are driving in a more secure environment than ever before.

And let's just address the obvious, which is a massive, built-in safety feature that for so many drivers doesn't come to mind: the mobile phone. Since price is no longer an object, virtually every driver out on the road has one—and on their daily commute, they're not necessarily aware that it's a safety tool for communicating in an emergency and it's a navigation device and it's a tracking device that police can use to find you. For these reasons, I recommend that you keep your smartphone out, plugged in, and available in your car. This does not mean you should look at texts and emails while you're driving—absolutely not. But you want it readily available in a dire situation. And that's not just for your personal emergency—the police's first line of defense is people calling 9-1-1. If you witness a collision, a crime, or something that's just not sitting right as you're driving, using a phone inside your car to call 9-1-1 is something that just didn't happen as recently as twenty years ago.

Smartphones and automatic locks are now a given in virtually every car, which has increased a sense of security out on the road. What do we need to make a conscious effort to remember to stay secure and safe in our cars?

If you're headed anywhere even the least bit unfamiliar to you, I would use a navigation app. You're apt to get there more quickly, which means a lower probability of an accident. You're also more likely not to get lost, which means less opportunity for bad actors to take advantage of you, and a higher probability that you'll stay in your car for the entire route—an option safer and more secure than needing to exit to get directions (or hey, use the facilities during a journey longer than it needed to be!).

Don't forget that these apps also typically report accidents, potholes, bad traffic, any number of things you might want to avoid. Plus, if anything ever happens to you, your use of the app is a way for some law enforcement to find and track you. Your phone, if on, is always transmitting your location—not always exactly, but law enforcement should be able to pinpoint your location within a few blocks.

God forbid, you lose control of the car, and suddenly you are in a ravine or a ditch, or off the road on a snowy day and you have to dial 9-1-1—you may not know where you are. You may be injured, you potentially may not know exactly what road you were on: The use of a mobile phone allows law enforcement to find you, and I've seen this be very successful in many rescues and many emergency situations in the past couple of years.

Nowadays cars that are coming off the line also have the ability to tell you if you're getting too close to a car or if another car is getting too close to you. So if you're backing up and you see a car behind you (because maybe you're in an SUV and the other car is a small sports car), you know because of that noise that one of you is getting too close.

Most cars nowadays have very sophisticated air bags and air bag systems—same with tires. Today, tires virtually never go flat instantaneously, giving you time to get to your destination and then address the problems. Many dashboards now will even tell you if your tire pressure is low. Blowouts are basically unheard of nowadays. The other amazing thing on cellphones today are the emergency, extreme weather, and AMBER alerts. That's the exact technology that police can use to triangulate your location, and it's the technology that gives you the knowledge you need to either avoid a situation or possibly help police save someone's life.

So when we take the entire modern car into consideration, people are inside very sophisticated machines thanks to auto manufacturers working alongside government safety regulations.

Do any of the massive leaps in progress for automobiles have a downside?

I wouldn't say downside—I would say trade-offs. You're less able today to manipulate the machinery yourself. As an ex-cop, I used to be able to use what they call a "slim jim" (a thin piece of metal that went between the window and the car door) after a distress call to get someone into or out of their locked cars—today, cars are too sophisticated to let anyone do that. For one thing, sometimes if you attempt to do this, the airbags go off. But the other side of that coin is that in many cases, I can call OnStar (or a similar service), and they can unlock the car from hundreds of miles away.

Remember, in an emergency, first responders will break your window to get you out if they need to—they won't be calling OnStar.

Overall, nowadays from a security standpoint you're much safer in your vehicle than you were twenty years ago.

So given this increased sort of no-thinking, built-in security, what do drivers and passengers still need to make an effort to do?

You have to put on your seat belts. You have to take the proper precautionary steps to keep yourself safe from the driver who is not driving safely—that means using your seat belt or not getting into the car in the first place.

I know better than anyone else that it is a very tempting thing to use your phone, to be distracted by your phone, to try to answer email or to read emails or read texts or answer texts while you're cruising around. I've seen firsthand—it really can cost you your life. Pull over if you have to. Put your hazards on, and make sure that you're in a safe position when you do pull over. Never, ever, ever while you're driving. Remember—at an average rate of speed, you are moving one football field every few seconds—so that's how far you can veer off course if you're distracted by your phone for just a few seconds. Looking down for a second or two could mean veering hundreds of yards. Don't even read your texts and emails, let alone answer them—it's not worth it.

By the same token, if you need to call someone, use the speaker phone and use your phone's features to use your voice to find and dial the contact. Just as in not texting and not emailing, I recommend never even dialing a number when you're driving. Again, pull over, dial the number, and then make the call on speaker.

If you have a medical or mechanical emergency, the first thing you should do is pull off to the side of the road, to the best of your ability, to the safest area you can find. What's a safe area? A good rule of thumb is making sure that you're more than half a car length away from the road or highway. Try not to leave your car if you don't have to, especially if you're in a deserted area. If this is a medical emergency, call 9-1-1. If you're having a mechanical emergency, you're always better off staying in the car or pulling the car off to the side of the road where your driver's side is the farthest from the road. That way, whether I stay inside or I get out of my car, the worst anyone could do is hit the left side of the car (which is important if I'm driving alone, but this tip isn't really practical for when I'm driving with passengers). It's simply a mindset to try to adopt when you're driving safely—what's the best way to pull over? If that means turning around and going in a different direction to get to the safer side of the road, so be it.

If you do need to exit your car (which I don't recommend in the majority of circumstances), your peripheral vision and awareness of traffic needs to be your number one priority. In countless cases, well-meaning people trying to make safe choices have been killed by exiting their pulled-over vehicle.

If you see an emergency unfolding:

You're better off either pulling off the road and making a 9-1-1 call, or making the 9-1-1 call on speaker and describing the scene to police as you keep going. Stopping and running across the highway can cost you your life. As an untrained civilian, it's not your job to go rescue someone, and possibly make the situation worse or more confusing for law enforcement.

Tell police what's happening; tell police what you see. Give them your full name and mobile phone number so they can contact you if they need additional information later that day or even later down the line as a witness or for information in a case. Call it in! Dial 9-1-1; do not call police departments directly. First, 9-1-1 is faster and more helpful to those in trouble, and second, your call is fully memorialized and able to be retrieved at a later date—this is not always the case for police departments. With enhanced 9-1-1 systems, even if your phone is private, your number will show up to the first responders.

Let's talk about running errands and driving in daily life.

For errands, park as close as you can to your destination's entrance. If it's late at night or dark, I like to park directly under a spotlight. If you're feeling insecure, putting your keys in between your fingers and forming a fist can serve as a defensive weapon. If assaulted, jabbing someone with those keys in the face or the chest might make them think twice about continuing to attack you. And just like while you're driving, keep your cellphone handy. Call a reliable friend; tell them where you are. Maybe an incident hasn't risen to the threshold of calling 9-1-1, but you want to let someone know where you are and what you're doing in case of escalation. In the same vein, there are apps that will show your family and friends exactly where you are—you might want to consider always having that feature turned on so that if, God forbid, something happens, five or more reliable people in your life can pinpoint your phone's location. There are also apps where, instead of calling 9-1-1, you press a button and those five or so contacts are alerted that you may need help. I recommend that all drivers research these apps and download and use the ones that they're comfortable with—new technology today could truly save your life.

If you feel that something in a parking lot situation is uncomfortable or off, you are much better off walking back into the store where there are other people than getting into your car. Stay where there are people if you feel the need. Don't hesitate to scream. Screaming "fire" is a great tool, because people will look over and be interested, as opposed to yelling "help," which many people tend to avoid or assume is arising from a personal, non-life-threatening disagreement in which they don't want to get involved.

Thomas Ruskin has been the president of the CMP Protective and Investigative Group, Inc., for the past decade. The CMP Group is an internationally recognized investigative and security firm with clients and corporations from around the world.

Mr. Ruskin is a highly decorated former New York City police detective investigator. He was responsible for crisis management for the mayor, police commissioner, and deputy commissioners of operations and crime control strategies for New York City. He has been involved in cases that have received worldwide attention, including the 1993 terrorist attack on the World Trade Center, the NYC subway system bombing, airline crashes, police shootings, hostage situations, and major organized crime and narcotics cases.

Mr. Ruskin's background includes responsibility for the protection of President Bill Clinton, Vice President Al Gore, Hillary Clinton, Tipper Gore, 1998 presidential candidate Senator Robert Dole, and other national and international dignitaries and heads of state. Mr. Ruskin has received specialized training from the NYPD Intelligence Division and the United States Secret Service in dignitary protection.

Mr. Ruskin is recognized as an international investigative, security, and crisis management expert by various news organizations including NBC, ABC, the Today show, Good Morning America, *CNN, Fox News Channel, and Sky News.*

NINJA TIPS: PARKING AND ENTERING

HERE'S A QUICK TIP to keep your car looking good, you healthy, and everyone safe: Whether it's food shopping, going to the mall, or taking in a football game, park your car farthest away from all the other cars as yours possibly can but, at the same time, in your line of sight. Why?

Security-wise, you have an unimpeded view of your car and anyone who could possibly be lurking around it, given the fact that you'll often park where there are no cars around you. Bad guys don't lurk around a car in a well-lit area. On a more minor note, this also prevents someone from dinging your car! And that walk will add more steps to your day—always a good thing.

When you approach your car (especially for the ladies), if you have mace or any protective weapon, I suggest having it within reach of your left hand so you can unlock and open the door with your right hand (of course, you can switch the dominant hands!).

Good habits are just as hard to break as bad habits. One day, a good habit may save you, and the irony is that these habits can save your life or your bodily integrity, without you even knowing it. The bad guys will not hide in or under your car, open it, or steal from it if it's alone and under a light.

BAD GUY POV: PREVENTING CAR THEFT

ACCORDING TO the National Highway Traffic Safety Administration, nearly half of car thefts could have been avoided if their drivers didn't make simple yet critical errors. They suggest you:

- ▸ Never leave your keys at, inside, or around your vehicle—always store them in a secure place or on your person.
- ▸ Lock all doors and close all windows whenever you exit your car.
- ▸ Hide any valuables you have to leave in your car (if you absolutely must leave them). Given the choice, you should err on the side of taking all valuables out of the car whenever you leave it.

COP CRIB NOTES:
SEE YOUR TRUNK AS YOUR UTILITY BELT

MOST PEOPLE VIEW the trunk of their car as a place to move and store luggage when they're going away for vacation. I look at the trunk of my car as its own version of Batman's utility belt . . . my meaning? If you were to look in the hatchback of my Audi SQ5 right now, I could pretty much guarantee you'd find virtually everything I need in case of an urban emergency, whether it be natural or man-made.

What do I have and why?

I have a portable battery charger, and a redundancy of items beyond that: jumper cables, water bottles, blankets, flares, reflective vests (if I EVER need to get out of my car at night), first aid kit, bungee cords, changes of clothes, rain poncho, spotlight, fix-a-flat, miniature shovel, umbrella, and even more. So why do I have all this? I'd rather have these items there and not need them than need them and not have them.

CHAPTER TEN

Detecting Deception

What Lies Ahead . . . Believing Can Be Quite Deceiving

WOULDN'T IT BE NICE to know when someone is lying to you? From white lies to life-altering fibs, we all might face a dozen tales of fiction a day. Believe it or not, the CIA has come impressively close to morphing into human lie-detectors by combining decades of research and in-the-field experience with some really, really bad people. I've spoken with my retired CIA sources, and to the extent that they can reveal their methods, this chapter is filled with tried-and-true techniques for revealing what we in the biz call "attempts at deception." After all, a "lie" can be an omission, a change of subject, or a refusal to answer honestly. If you acquaint yourself with the logic behind these procedures—which I spell out in this chapter—whether it's a date or a job review, you'll go in armed and prepared.

STANTON STORY

COMING FROM A GUY whose initials are B.S., you might think I'd be the last guy to reveal the tricks of the trade to detecting deception, right? Wrong! My black belt in B.S. (used only when absolutely necessary, of course)—and my monogram—means I'm the best guy to tell you how to sniff it out.

I could get into the weeds about my inherent B.S. meter or tell you how I triangulate in on a liar. But I'd rather give you access to the best cache of tools money can buy . . . QVerity.

It's a company whose founding members are from "The Company," or as it's more commonly known, the CIA. Their skill set, when you really break it down? The Detection of Deception. Phil Houston, my business partner at QVerity and its CEO, developed his second-to-none technique over the course of his twenty-five-year career at the spook shop. Our partners Susan and Mike round out the rest of the team, and when huge corporations or foreign interests need to find out who's lying to them and who's telling the truth, we're called in.

We work with normal individuals, high-net-worth clients, law enforcement agencies, attorneys, news networks, and hedge funds. In essence, for those who appreciate and understand the true value of the actual ability to detect deception, it's *Moneyball* for the private sector. When analyzing business deals, politics, sports, and crimes, we've found that anyone who can get away with telling a lie that benefits them will very often lie. Sad, but it's just what the research tells us.

When people's lives, livelihoods, and even their love lives are possibly affected by deceptive practices, we get the call. Trained by my partners at QVerity, who literally wrote the book on how to *Spy the Lie*, I'll teach you how to read verbal as well as nonverbal indicators. When someone inevitably tells you, "Believe me when I tell you . . . ," can you, actually?

Think about it for a minute. Wouldn't the very ability to accurately detect deception be a great addition to your Super-Semi-Top-Secret-Ninja-PI-Spy tool kit? In this age where kids grow up too fast, and the internet is all easily accessible, it can be as simple as how you approach (and how confident you feel after) confronting your kids, hoping for truthful answers. I'll teach you to observe less closely the words they're saying and focus more importantly on how they're saying it.

When you ask your boss about your future in the company (as he or she assures you they'd never lie to you and how you're destined for a promotion), can you really trust their feedback?

After reading this chapter, you might just discover it's time to get your résumé ready—and QVerity and I come up with these techniques not for the sake of revealing a painful truth, but because the reality is that you will lead a better life with the truth—knowledge—at your fingertips. Forget jobs for a moment; family is likely more important. When interviewing the elderly care attendant for your mother, wouldn't you prefer to have the ability to detect deceptive indicators when they speak about their past experiences?

Frankly, this chapter will show you which people in your life to kick to the curb. You'll know that you can't let this person come one inch closer to your elderly mother, regardless of their sweet bedside manner. These tried-and-true techniques, tested by Harvard, will help you throughout your life.

LIES are like potential land mines, and this chapter is your bomb-sniffing (B.S.) DOG!

Late 1980s. New York City . . . I am in flux by way of my career. I am working for an investigation company doing surveillance and security details, which I will tell you is infinitesimally boring—nothing at all like it is in the movies. Also unlike the movies, I had to supplement my income by being a nightclub bouncer—where, ironically, I was shot at and stabbed far more frequently than I ever was in the NYPD.

During this time, I was searching for direction, hoping to up my game and become more than just "the guy with the list at the club" or "the guy who sat in front of a house for twenty hours waiting for someone to show up." While looking for direction and purpose, I was offered an opportunity through an acquaintance. The opportunity? See a high-level CIA agent speak on detecting deception. This sounded somewhat security related, so I bit. Being fearful and a tad insecure, I asked my acquaintance if I could take some of my well-credentialed friends along with me—it turns out, as I dug into the specifics, that speech was more of an interactive course than listening to an expert. As luck would have it, the "course" was right by the CIA headquarters in Langley, Virginia—this felt like it had gravitas, and I was excited.

Through force of will and using every ounce of persuasion, calling in every favor I could call in, I rounded up a group of friends to come with me. The three amigos? John Miller, former award-winning journalist and currently the deputy commissioner of counter-terrorism for NYPD, now-retired NYPD chief John Fehey, and last but not least, one of the best police detectives I've ever worked with, Mike Swain (also now retired). All three had phenomenal credentials at the time in investigation in their own right—different backgrounds, running the gamut from journalism to interrogation.

Their take? Sure, we'll come, but can we learn that much when we're already at the top at our investigative game?

I will tell you, at the end of that eight-hour seminar, the Kool-Aid was flowing, and it was easy to drink. Why? The man who made and created this course. The man was Phil Houston. Phil is a legend in his field—he created and now teaches the art of detecting deception. From that time to this writing, I have become his friend, his student, and currently his business partner. I am proudly his grasshopper. Phil Houston is the master ninja at spying the lie.

What he's taught me? Keep reading.

I'd like to take a moment and say that while, arguably, every chapter in this book is important, possibly the most important is the one you're reading now. Why? Because learning this skill is almost like gaining a super power. What I want to touch upon is that bad guys don't always wear a shirt that says, "I'm out to get you." As we've tragically seen in the news and in the tabloids, bad guys can come in the disguise of a good person: from priests to babysitters, to even a trusted relative. Bad guys are all too often in sheep's clothing—which is why we catch them too late much of the time. With this chapter, and learning what's inside it, you could possibly see predators before they prey, and when they're still dressed as a sheep instead of the wolves they are.

BUT FIRST, YOU NEED TO KNOW . . .

▶ If you ask the average American if they've lied in the last twenty-four hours, 40 percent will say yes.

▶ Research shows that "white lies" are more common than "important" lies.

▶ The majority of lies are told by a minority of "prolific liars."

▶ Many of the things we assume about how to spot a liar are false but pervasive. For example, a majority of people across cultures think that when a person lies, they don't make eye contact, or they avert their gaze. But there's no concrete evidence that suggests that's the case—especially because many don't make full eye contact in totally truthful conversations.

STREET SMARTS: FINE-TUNING YOUR "B.S." RADAR

The biggest mistake we make when we are deceived is allowing our biases to obscure the truth that's playing out right before our eyes. Without realizing it, we're being significantly influenced by preconceived notions of what to expect. And so unless we recognize that and say to ourselves, "I'm going to be as objective as I can possibly be," we don't have a place to start.

Now we just can't tell ourselves to be objective and expect our brains to do that. All right. So what we have to do is follow a formula or a set of rules that forces us to become aware of deception.

Step to Success: Ignore What Sounds Good to You

The first rule here is simple but it can be difficult: Ignore what sounds good to you.

Let's say I really like a person, then all of a sudden she says or he says, "Bill, I know what a great investigator you are." I need to ignore that comment. Now, it could be genuine. But it could also be designed to butter me up and lead me astray.

Let's say the person you know appears calm and relaxed—that's a behavior that sounds and looks good. So again, we need to ignore that. A calm demeanor may be natural, but it may be contrived as well. Again, ignore what looks good.

Deception Indicator: Evasion

Be on the lookout for specific deceptive indicators. Those indicators can be found in broad categories. The first big one is evasion. When people are evasive, it typically means that they've decided not to provide us with the information we've asked for or are looking for. So how does that manifest itself? They don't answer our questions. They talk around it, or the way they might hide something is such a blatant attempt to hide it that what's missing becomes obvious. For example, if I said, "Did you rob the bank?" they may spend so much time explaining why they couldn't have robbed it that they never actually answer "no." Look for evasion in non-answers.

Deception Indicator: Persuasion

Watch for a person who is trying to convince rather than trying to convey: When you ask someone a question and, rather than giving you the only answer you're asking for, they're adding unnecessary information. So let's stay with the bank-robbing example, I ask, "Did you rob the bank?"—and in the case of a persuader, they might tell me "no" straight off the bat, but then try to convince me as to why they would never make such an immoral decision. "I'm an honest person, and I don't want to go to jail." Persuasion is indeed an indicator of someone attempting to deceive you.

We call these "convincing statements." People try to get us to believe their side of the story in a variety of ways, but convincing statements are the most powerful. The person transforms before our eyes to the salesperson who's trying to sell us something, moving right into sales mode. When evasion behavior is coupled with persuasion, we know the speaker knows he's trying to sell us a lemon.

Deception Indicator: Aggression

Aggression occurs when the person you're questioning has become so concerned about you finding out the truth that they try to get you to back off, and they immediately become aggressive. "I can't believe you would ever ask me something like that!" "I thought you knew me better than that!" "Why would you ask that?"

They either attack you, or they attack the situation. "I can't believe this questioning is taking so long." Or they might attack a third party: "Well, he always has lies," or, "Well, that company's never liked me," or "How on earth would they know?"

Deception Indicator: Manipulation

Lying is difficult for most people—some people are better at lying than others, but sometimes it's a little bit difficult. One reason it's difficult is that when someone asks the question they expect an answer on a fairly timely basis. When a person is lying, often the person has think of how they're going to lie, and so in order to do that, they have to buy themselves some time. And to go back to our bank robbing, they might repeat the question: "Did I rob the bank?"

We sometimes refer to them as non-answer statements. "Well, that's a good question."

Deception Indicator: Nonverbal Cues

One is the inappropriate pause. Let's say I ask you this question: "What were you doing on January twenty-second, five years ago?" You'd probably have to pause to think about that, right? Yes. However, if I asked, "On January twenty-second, five years ago, did you rob a bank that day?" If you pause with a long, "Ummmmmm, let me think . . . ," that pause is inappropriate. Now, that's a particularly obvious example, but this can crop up in your personal life as well. "Junior, I saw on your social media feed that you were posting from a concert. Did you really go to the library last night?"

Let's go to another nonverbal indicator, and let's keep in mind that lying is hard for most people. We're worried that the other person can see right through us. So many times, in the process of lying we start to groom ourselves. We brush our hair, tug on our ear, rub our nose, any kind of grooming. We might start to adjust our clothing. We may even start to groom the surroundings a little bit, like we brush something off the desk or off the table, or move our coffee cup a little bit, or tidy up what's directly in front of us.

More Than One Deception Indicator May Point to Lying

If just one indicator is present, the person could be telling the truth. But as the number of indicators grows, deception is more likely to be occurring.

While no one is a human lie detector, our combined decades of experience tells us these indicators are highly accurate most of the time.

CHAPTER ELEVEN

Interacting with Law Enforcement

Lesson One: Put Yourself in the Cop's Shoes

EVERY DAY IN THE NEWS, there seems to be a new story of a civilian dying or rendered grievously injured by the police. As a former officer myself, I can attest that there are a few bad apples in every bunch. While you can only control YOU, keep reading for advice straight from good cops on how to de-escalate any police-involved situation you might find yourself in. My two cents? Get that bad-apple cop back in the courts or with a video on social media... not in the moment. Here's how.

STANTON STORY

I'M IN MY LATE TWENTIES and a few years post my NYPD days. I've grown my hair rock-star long and I'm loving life, tooling down a long stretch of highway heading to Aspen, Colorado, for a dream job opportunity. You see, the China Club was the HOTTEST nightclub in the world and yours truly was offered to run the door at their newest Aspen outpost.

Yep, it was a good day, and slowly but surely eighty mph crept up to ninety mph, crept up to one hundred mph. I couldn't wait to get to my new life. I'm singing along to a cassette mixtape that even *Guardians of the Galaxy* would envy, when seemingly out of nowhere I see strobe lights in my rearview. Yep, Wild Bill was caught getting a little too wild while singing along to the Eagles hit . . . you guessed it: "Life in the Fast Lane."

"Not to worry," I say to myself, as I put on my hazards and roll onto the shoulder. I'm ex-NYPD and I'll explain it away to this Denver state trooper.

I'm looking through my sideview mirror, and out pops what I'd describe as a NFL offensive lineman in a leather jacket and boots straight out of *Mad Max*. (Or at least, that was my perception as he boldly approached my 1988 Nissan Pathfinder with New York vanity plates proclaiming H1GHNOON).

As the giant trooper peered into my window to make sure I was alone (before I had a chance to dazzle him with my charming wit, of course—and what some have called my "black belt in bullshit") he bluntly demanded, "License and registration." No please. . . nothing. No chance for me to explain, or to show off my police veteran status.

"OK," I thought, "time for plan B." Back in those days, I carried my license in my courtesy-shield case, right next to a smaller version of my old NYPD badge and ID card. In my mind, once he saw that gleaming shield, we'd be brothers in arms, right? WRONG!

That fricking trooper, clearly seeing the shield, grabs my driver's license as soon as my two fingers can pull it out of the case. Then he says, "Wait here." Wait here? WTF, I say to myself, full of self-entitlement! Knowing that he clearly knows I'm formerly "on the job," I get out of my Pathfinder, wearing my own biker jacket and cowboy boots (hey, I was heading to Aspen after all) when I semi-shout out and say, "Excuse me—in New York City we show fellow officers courtesy." The trooper stops dead in his tracks, about half-way between my car and his. For two heartbeats he stands there, me staring at his lunar eclipse–sized back, and on a dime he pivots. Between walking and running, he charges me! Grabbing my lapels, he lifts me off my feet and throws me back into my car, slamming the door shut! Looking in my window, and pointing his finger, he says, "Shut the f*** up and don't f***ing move!"

Clearly, the combination of him having a bad day mixed with my hubris didn't make for the best *Dancing with the Stars* team.

Upon his return, I shifted attitude gears, going full Beta Male, belly up, white flag out, as I profusely apologized for speeding, etc.

Now some would (and perhaps should) make an argument that the trooper was abusive. We can debate that for another time. But for the time being, I'd rather like to discuss how everyday Americans can best serve themselves as well as the brave police men and -women across the country . . . and that all comes down to how you interact with them and respond to them—whether they are acting in your best interests or not.

BUT FIRST, YOU NEED TO KNOW . . .

The most common interaction a civilian has with a law enforcement officer is a traffic stop.

- ▸ Twelve percent of drivers are pulled over each year.
- ▸ Drivers say speeding was most often the reason police claimed they were getting pulled over.
- ▸ Three percent of stops lead to searches. A Hispanic driver is most likely to be searched.
- ▸ Male drivers are more likely to be pulled over than female drivers.
- ▸ Black drivers are more likely to be pulled over than Hispanic or white drivers.

Nearly one thousand people were fatally shot by police in 2017. Seven percent of those people were not armed. Forty-six police officers were murdered in the line of duty. According to the *Washington Post*'s database, when it comes to fatal police shootings:

- ▸ Forty-four percent were white males; three hundred and thirty were armed (about 76 percent of those killed).
- ▸ Twenty-two percent were black males; one hundred sixty were armed (about 74 percent of those killed); nineteen were unarmed.
- ▸ Eighteen percent were Hispanic males.
- ▸ Sixteen percent were female.

About fifty-one thousand people go to the emergency room and are injured every year by encounters with police.

In January 2017, Pew Research released a survey with troubling results if our goal is that police and civilians be on the same page and respect one another:

- ▸ Ninety-three percent of officers say they are more concerned about their safety in the wake of high-profile incidents involving black victims.

- Sixty-seven percent of police say fatal encounters with black people are isolated incidents, but 60 percent of the public say those encounters are signs of a broader problem.

- Ninety-two percent of white officers say our country has made the appropriate changes to give different races equal rights, while only 29 percent of black police officers feel that way. Of the general public, only 69 percent of people say our country has made the appropriate changes to give different races equal rights.

- Eighty-six percent of police officers think the general public doesn't understand the risks they face.

EXPERT INTERVIEW
A High-Ranking Officer in the NYPD

Tell us your perception. As an active-duty police chief, what is the average man-on-the-street's attitude toward police?

There are multiple YouTube videos that show police–civilian encounters—and my take is that in not all but some of these interactions, people have been what I call "trained by TV." And then, the YouTube viewers absorb what they see, and that trickles into their interactions with and perceptions of police. Because of the nature of television ratings, the most aggressive and most upsetting clips are shown over and over again—and civilians can become much more agitated than they might be under other circumstances with police work. In my experience, the confrontational nature of the people being targeted has risen tremendously. Ninety-eight percent of the population, if not more, are tremendously respectful of police officers. If you're not dealing with a bad-apple cop, that goes a long way.

Any cop will tell you, on patrol, one of the worst things you can hear is a parent talking to a child acting up: "If you keep this up—see that police officer?—I'll call them and have them take you away . . . or, I'll call and have them come over and set you straight." We don't want to be disciplinarians, and we don't want children to grow up associating us with punishment and/or fear. You want people to know that we're the people you go to for help. We are not an occupying army, and we shouldn't be.

What are police thinking, where is their head, when they're out on the job?

Nearly every police officer goes into police work to protect and serve. If you ask a police officer why this is their career, they won't tell you, "I really like the action." They did it to help their community, probably hoping against hope that there's no action. That doesn't mean we always do it right; that doesn't mean they don't make mistakes. That doesn't mean police never act on misinformation. In some ways, I wonder why police encounters don't go wrong more often, given that these are two human beings who are imperfect in one of the most intense moments they'll ever have, for either one of them.

In New York City, and some highly populated cities across the country, police got a rap for bringing down crime in the 1990s by being aggressive. Well, we've moved on from that. With overall crime rates successfully decreasing, you'll find that most law enforcement has switched gears to what we call a community policing model. New York Police Department's Commissioner O'Neill has also talked about a concept called "precision policing." Instead of throwing a big net over an area, you're looking specifically to identify and address those people who are causing harm to that community. That's the current trend in New York law enforcement—toward precision policing. That revamp starts with "neighborhood policing"—getting to the point, you hope, with your community that someone is willing to call you if they're in trouble.

Let me explain a type of encounter I've had a few times that's upsetting but seemingly unavoidable. A call comes over the radio: "Suspect, rape, white male, six one, two hundred fifty pounds, jeans and white T-shirt, has a gun, consider armed and dangerous." My guys might tackle to the ground any white man in the area who happens to be about that size and in jeans and any variation of white shirt. That could be six 100 percent innocent men that day, and they leave the police encounter with bruises, shock, and perhaps the absolutely single-most-terrifying encounter of their life. If this guy starts throwing punches or mouthing off, coupled with a few rookie police officers thinking that a) this guy has a gun, and b) this guy just raped someone, this encounter could go south very quickly for a man who happens to be completely innocent. We understand that most people are completely innocent—this chapter is not a pie-in-the-sky improbability. At some point in your life, you will probably interact with police.

OK, let's take three scenarios, and let's talk about what a person can do to make this encounter go as smoothly as possible: You're a victim of a crime, you appear to be accused of a crime, or you're in your car and getting pulled over.

As Americans, we've all been taught to question authority, and that's a great thing. But there's a certain way to question authority and a time and place to question authority. Questioning authority is more productive than seething contempt for authority. You are absolutely entitled to verbally abuse a police officer. Safety and security aren't always in the realm of what your God-given, Constitution-given rights are. I am trying to teach you what will most likely help you in that moment, and it's not always what you have the absolute right to do.

STREET SMARTS:
WHAT NOT TO SAY TO A POLICE OFFICER
IF YOU WANT TO DE-ESCALATE

▶ "Who are you to tell me what to do?!"

▶ "You don't get to tell me where I go or what I can't say."

▶ "I pay your salary!"

▶ Cursing at the cop or calling him or her an asshole

▶ "You have nothing better to do?"

▶ "You're talking to me when there are actual criminals out there?"

PEOPLE constantly challenge cops in the street. A good cop, a good egg will not react negatively to that. But here's some advice to make sure you come out of the encounter alive and well. Let's say a cop, working on misinformation perhaps, thinks you are a suspect and thinks you are resisting arrest. Generally, raising your voice and adding fighting words to that mix of already being suspected is not going to calm an aggressive cop.

The best advice, whether you're pulled over or whether you get stopped on the street because you resemble the description of a suspect, is this: Acquiesce with orders to the best of your comfort level. Why? You are not going to win a battle of wits, words, or physicality out on the street. Even if you think that cop is 100 percent wrong, hold your fire for administrative or legal avenues. If it's in your head that cops are corrupt and criminal, shouldn't you employ the same strategic thinking you'd use if you were being attacked by a criminal? How would you deal with a criminal who's attacking you? You probably wouldn't curse him out and start physically fighting him if he has a firearm and backup, unless you were in immediate fear for your life. There are different venues for winning the confrontation than the in-the-moment venue. If you feel you were treated badly by a police officer, any number of pro bono lawyers would be looking to take on that high-profile case. Especially today, many police encounters are recorded by onlookers or even by the police themselves. But that brings up another common escalation: The cop demands to see your hands, and you're fumbling around for your cellphone to record the encounter—that officer is trained to think you're looking for a weapon. Be smart about this.

Let's talk about getting pulled over.

Let's make this really simple because this is the encounter that's most likely to happen to our readers. Putting yourself in the cop's shoes, remember that you could have been pulled over for something as minor as being ten miles per hour over the speed limit, or for something as major as resembling a suspect of a murder, even though you're innocent. The point is that the officer might be approaching your vehicle with a great deal of tension.

COP CRIB NOTES: AN OFFICER APPROACHES YOUR CAR. HERE'S WHAT TO DO . . .

- At a minimum, turn off the radio—I'd go so far as to turn off the entire engine.
- Roll down the window.
- At a minimum, place both hands on the steering wheel. One next-level move is resting both of your empty hands outside the window. If nothing else, this signals to the officer that you're cooperative, or that you know police and have asked what they recommend you do after being pulled over.
- Once the officer approaches, ask him if you should stay inside or exit the vehicle (different states have different procedures).
- If it's dark out, turn on all of your car's interior lights to show that you have nothing to hide and that you are cooperating.

You and the Officer Are Talking

The officer will probably ask to see your license and registration. Unless you have these items in your lap, you will need to move your hands to get these. I recommend telling, then asking before you do anything: "I think my license is in my purse—do you mind if I turn around to get it in the backseat?" Or, "My registration is in my glove compartment—can I open the glove compartment and get it out?"

I would recommend not making a movement without explaining it first.

Police officers do have some level of discretion on whether or not they write a summons. The sure way to move yourself into summons territory is to argue with the police officer, starting out with "I can't believe I'm getting pulled over when my tax dollars pay your salary." That may not be right, but it's what I've observed to be reality. By the same token, an officer may have been told that morning by his chief that he has no discretion out on the road: "I don't care if it's a mini-van with five kids in it, if it's going a mile over the speed limit, you write them a ticket." So, my advice isn't aimed at how to get out of a ticket. I'm trying to give you insight into what cops are working with so that you can keep yourself and the people in your car as safe as possible.

We tell our cops to start an encounter at the most relaxed, polite, calm level possible, because you can always ramp up if the situation warrants that. What's really hard to do is to bring an encounter back to normal, back to civil. Once you escalate, it's really hard to come back down.

When You Call Police

Let's talk about how to reach out to police and interact with police when you're a victim or survivor of a crime.

My most important piece of advice would be to let go of all feelings of shame and embarrassment and tell us the whole story. I can't tell you how many times we could have solved the crime more quickly and saved future victims if we had known more from the first victim who came forward. A common example: A rapist uses a dating app for predation. Many survivors have been embarrassed to even tell a detective, "I met him on Tinder, we chatted on the site, and then I met him in person at Starbucks." With a detail like that, we could probably track down the suspect much more quickly and efficiently.

Survivors of sexual assault and misconduct, of course, can also be male, and we want men to tell us everything as well. Are you married, perhaps to a woman, and worried that this will get out? First, we can't disclose anything about survivors without their permission, and second, there's a rapist out there we're trying to catch. There's no judgment here—as police, our job is to make sure this doesn't happen to anyone else.

Another victim that's typically embarrassed to come forward or to share every detail is the victim of a scam. You send a bad actor your banking information? Credit card numbers? Your password? A nude photo? In police work, we're seeing cybercrime and cyberscamming more and more often.

For a generation of Americans that I see as compassionate and willing to help others, one scam I see that's becoming more and more common is someone saying: "I have a few thousand dollars, but I am unable to declare it in the United States because I'm an undocumented immigrant. Could you give me a few thousand dollars to hire a lawyer and get the process started, and then I'll give you X amount of dollars?"

Don't be embarrassed—please, give us the information we need to catch this person.

Tell us your most frustrating recent encounter as a police officer.

I will go back to an overriding theme of both how to interact with police and what police run into out on the job: Just because you have the right to do something does not mean that it's a prudent (read: safe and secure) choice.

I was recently driving slowly through Central Park very early in the morning—at about 5:00 a.m., so it was practically still dark out. I was in a large police SUV—so we're talking about a roughly two- to three-ton vehicle. I happen upon a woman dressed completely in black, with earbuds in, and I expect her to look around, acknowledge me, and move over just a bit from the car. Well, those must have been noise-canceling earphones, because she didn't hear the car at all. Eventually I waved her down and suggested that for running in near darkness, she use regular headphones or keep just one earbud in, noting that she didn't even hear my SUV.

Instead of agreeing, she appeared agitated, telling me that she can do whatever she wants. That's absolutely true, and that's her right. But this is exactly the sitting duck that predators look for. If you can't hear an SUV a few feet from you with the amazing new earphones companies are putting out, you are not going to hear a human being approaching you.

Did my approach change her mind or her future actions? Probably not. And that's what frustrates me as a member of law enforcement—you try to make slight, proactive changes so that you can truly "protect and serve." That doesn't always make a difference.

CHAPTER TWELVE

Illicit Drugs

What to Do When They Enter Your Life

YOU'VE SEEN THE HEADLINES . . . America is in the midst of a national emergency, and a crisis of the soul, when it comes to misusing drugs—and that doesn't seem to be ending anytime soon. Nationwide, government-sponsored research suggests that one in ten Americans has used a dangerous, mind-altering drug in the last month. Since the War on Drugs of the 1980s, we've come so far in realizing what does and doesn't work to keep people away from hurting themselves with substances . . . and one of the keys to success is avoiding moral judgment. This chapter does exactly that, from pot to opioids. Inside, you'll find the latest stats and expert advice, all to help kick off a healthy, safe lifestyle.

STANTON STORY

WHILE I WAS RAISED in a working-class, blue-collar family, during my early years, I was led to believe that drugs were absolutely forbidden and evil. It was only later that I came to realize that my father and his friends, during the 1970s, indulged in pot and, my guess would be, other drugs as well. I remember the anger I felt when I found out, which only strengthened my resolve to never do drugs, and to become a cop. During my short tenure in the NYPD, I was a first-hand witness to the devastating effects of heroin on the minority communities in lower-income neighborhoods. Back then, I was young, impressionable, and myopic in my view, wrongfully thinking that these folks got what they had coming to them, because they tried drugs, and everyone tells you not to do drugs. These folks always looked like extras on the set of *The Walking Dead*—zombies lying down or stumbling around an abandoned building.

After being forced to retire after my injury, I ended up living in Aspen, Colorado, to be a bouncer at the China Club, one of the hottest clubs of the 1990s. Now, in this chapter of my life, the China Club, instead of the NYPD, became my community. It was ground zero for every celeb, etc.

At the China Club, I saw the other end of the American drug story. Let's just say rich, famous people really let their hair down, engaging in substances that were neither legal nor prescribed by a doctor. My first knee-jerk reaction was thinking, "What hypocrites." But upon reflection, I thought: These are grown-up adults who pay their bills. If they want to indulge, what makes them wrong and me right, when I'm staying within the bounds of legality ... but drinking way too many vodka shots for my own good.

So, if I sound like I'm all over the place on this subject—it's because I am, and my opinion is still evolving on this very complicated issue (as is America's opinion, it would seem). But one place I remain stalwart is drugs and children. Like makeup, fast food, and cars, drugs is a business aimed at hooking teenagers—and in America, business is booming. And since drugs aren't regulated like cigarettes, alcohol, and yes, even makeup—and oh, by the way, drugs can't be in TV commercials—sales and marketing for these unregulated products starts in grade school and is intense.

While there are more so-called professionals that feel they have the answer to how to stop this, my feeling is, there is no magic pill to stop kids from taking pills—the messaging ultimately begins and ends in the home. Parents in today's culture seem all too eager to be their children's friends and shoulder-shrug the dangers of today. "I did it, so how can I tell them not to?" I'm telling you, BE THE HYPOCRITE. Drugs have become so much more potent and available than they ever were in our day. Today, there are no "phases." "Oh I had a pot phase." OK, guess what? There are no heroin phases. There are no meth phases. You try, you're addicted, you die.

And unlike our day, drug addiction is not limited to outliers and communities with a lower income. Today, we can truly say that addiction is raceless, classless, and genderless. Whether it's a hand-off of crack in an elementary school playground, or Percocet in the medicine cabinet of your mother's bathroom, way too many children are dying because of lack of education and awareness around drugs, and all the forms they come in.

So, I will direct those reading this chapter to check out our Detection of Deception chapter of just one way to (to quote President

Ronald Reagan) "trust but verify" what your children are doing. We'll also outline warning signs that your child is using drugs, as well as other ways to figure out if your kid is getting stoned, without necessarily having to interrogate them. One way that immediately comes to my mind is to (yes, it sounds crazy) take a hair from their hairbrush, take it to your pharmacy, and mail in a drug kit to companies that will tell you what drugs your child is using (or no drugs at all, as the case may be)—without you ever having to confront your child, especially if something seems off. Then, you confront them with facts from a lab instead of your own speculations. It's tough to argue with that.

But I digress. My bottom line? Just because a doctor writes you a prescription doesn't mean you should feel obligated to fill it.

BUT FIRST, YOU NEED TO KNOW . . .

The latest stats from the National Institute on Drug Abuse (NIDA):

- In 2015, more than thirty-three thousand Americans died as a result of any kind of opioid overdose—this number is about equal to how many Americans die each year from gun violence. Ask yourself: Are you more fearful of a firearm killing you or a loved one than opioids doing the same? Keep in mind that the statistics are very similar there, but gun violence gets far more attention in the media.

- An estimated two million Americans abuse opioids.

- Nearly one in three of those who get a LEGAL prescription for an opioid pain reliever go on to abuse the drug, either seeking out prescription drugs illegally or moving over to heroin or other street opioids.

- About 80 percent of heroin users first misused prescription opioids.

- About one in twenty people who misuse prescription opioids eventurally turn to heroin.

The latest stats from the Centers for Disease Control and Prevention (CDC) holds this shocking information:

- Every day, an average of one hundred thirty Americans die from an opioid overdose.

- There was no good reason for opioid prescription numbers to increase, because we now know that Americans did not report any more pain than they did in the past. All of this raises questions as to whether doctors were pushing painkillers—all legal, but perhaps scarily immoral.

- The amount of prescription opioids sold to pharmacies, hospitals, and doctors' offices nearly quadrupled from 1999 to 2010.

- Deaths from prescription opioids—drugs like oxycodone, hydrocodone, and methadone—have more than quadrupled since 1999.

- Among new heroin users, approximately three out of four reported abusing prescription opioids prior to using heroin.

EXPERT INTERVIEW
Dr. Jane Fitzgerald

Can you speak about some ways you can avoid getting addicted to begin with and then perhaps if you do come into the clutches of addiction, what you can do naturally to help solve the issue?

This has gotten so much attention now, and I think thanks in part to President Trump. I think many cases of opioid addiction, and even heroin use, can be traced back to an epidemic of chronic back pain in America that for too long was treated improperly. That pain has actually been identified as one of the most common reasons why a primary care physician prescribes opioids—which is not the route I might first take when someone comes to me with back pain.

A lot of research has been done on this phenomenon, and a compilation of some of that research, from the *Journal of the American Medical Association* in 2016, suggests that most of these drugs are essentially ineffective for treating chronic low back pain.

So, not only are you taking a drug where you could become addicted, but on top of that, that drug alone might not even work to fix your back pain?

Correct. And I think a way to avoid it is mass education to everybody who deals with these pain sufferers who you know. Explain to them that they have to look for non-pharmacological intervention for pain treatment as a first step. This concept of non-opioid therapies first, then prescribing opioids as a last resort, is backed up by my own experience in the field and in the ways our country is coming to grips with the opioid crisis.

We're seeing the cost-effectiveness of chiropractic versus medical treatment and medical management of a low back pain sufferer. We're talking roughly $1,500 for chiropractic treatment, compared to $7,000 for medical management. The patients are getting better with non-pharmacological intervention. One of the strongest ways to avoid addiction is education. If you know that to help avoid addiction, the first place to start is with natural modalities, like chiropractic, like massage therapy, like acupuncture, like nutrition, like exercise and lifestyle modification, you will be better armed. I'm a big proponent of the idea that prevention is the best cure for a lot of things.

Most of the time, our pain comes from inflammation, and there are so many things that people can do to try to decrease pain before they reach for a pill. For my patients, I've found that white sugar, white flour, alcohol, caffeine, and nicotine are all going to increase your pain. You could try applying an ice pack, taking an Epsom salt baths, or just doing some deep breathing, reading, or listening to uplifting music. Try all of these things first before visiting a doctor who might prescribe you an opioid.

Got it. Let's say someone has tried all that, and they're still facing excruciating pain. What step should they take to manage that pain?

Well, I always tell my patients: Look, we could always ramp this up. The Joint Commission, the organization that accredits more than twenty thousand health care systems in the United States, is recognizing the value of adding non-drug approaches like chiropractic and acupuncture to pain management—and the idea of taking that route first is becoming more commonplace.

If those treatments provide little or no relief, ask your doctor if you should move on to medications and possibly injections. The power of taking non-opioid steps to manage pain first is that those steps are either going to help you or they're going to do nothing. The average risk of any side effects is exceptionally low. The danger of grabbing a pill is that it might not help you, and then along with not being helped, you could become addicted.

Hopefully our current crisis has opened a lot of people's eyes. I know that I personally have become much more aware of how chronic both pain and opioid addiction are, even in the last few months. Your doctors need to work together as a team. They should be looped in with each other, and you the patient should be a full member of that team.

Dr. Jane Fitzgerald graduated from New York Chiropractic College in 1990 and has been practicing in the Bronx for nearly three decades.

CHAPTER THIRTEEN

Pets

When the Going Gets Ruff Ruff... Pet Safety and Security

THEY'RE BY OUR SIDE through good times and bad. They love us at our worst, which makes them the best. For most, our pets are not the "property" the law views them as. Rather, they're our family (and sometimes the best-behaved members!), our children to be nurtured and protected from harm.

I'm lucky enough that back in the day, Steve Diller, the renowned animal behaviorist, signed on as trainer to my king shepherd Bishop (RIP) and Teddy Bear Goldendoodle Lucy. Once he said to me, "There's no such thing as a bad dog, as much as bad owners." No truer words can be spoken.

If you are one of the millions of pet owners or you're a human tempted to buy or adopt a pet, I recommend reading this chapter to consider the responsibility and knowledge that your pet (or potential pet) relies on you for. You owe your pet constant guidance, sustenance, protection, and love.

In turn you'll receive the same . . . but in different ways. This chapter will only strengthen your unique bond, ensuring a lifetime of memories that both you and your pet will cherish.

Subtopics:

- ▶ Aggressive dog attack
- ▶ Walking your dog safely, for the dog and the pedestrian
- ▶ Dognapping
- ▶ Dogs in vehicles
- ▶ Children and dogs

STANTON STORY

For those who are religious, besides the gifts of free will and opposable thumbs, God's greatest gift to us is the dog. I don't seek to diminish the cat lovers, the bird lovers, and those who love all other creatures . . . but for me, the dog is the be-all and end-all. And in this story, it's my Bishop: a stunning king shepherd, and my darling Lucy, a Teddy Bear Goldendoodle.

During our adventures, many of the lessons and tips I'm about to give come from experience with these two, ranging from my hand almost being bitten off by a pit bull, to my big boy jumping onto a delivery person (none of us wants to get sued as a result of our pet), to people leaving dogs in hot cars, and folks walking their dogs off-leash. The main thrust of this chapter will be: There's no such thing as a bad dog (or pet)—just bad owners.

Know what you need in a pet versus what you (think) you want, and know how to manage those expectations, as well as that beautiful creature that you'll bring into your home.

One tragic tail—pun intended—happened as I was on my way home from the gym one night, turning onto my street. I see a man whom I often see with his dogs. This man is nearly seven feet tall and three hundred pounds. He is hard to miss, since he always has a small basset hound and a small poodle trailing behind him. On this particular day, as I turned the corner, I saw him lying on the ground, with half of his body on the sidewalk and half on the street.

The man held his head in his arms and there was a trail of blood behind him in the street. My first thought was that he had either been shot in the head or someone had taken a bat to him. I immediately pulled over and jumped out of my car, and as soon as I got out, I could hear him wailing in pain. I tentatively approached him (along with others) to check his injuries (blood was now streaming down the sidewalk). Upon close inspection, I came to realize that it wasn't his blood.

This man was wailing in the street, head down, in deepest despair, because his small poodle had been hit by a car. No one deserves this, but it is the reasonably foreseeable outcome of not walking your dogs on a leash.

I sat with that man, hand on his back, for more than an hour, trying to console him. His deceased best friend lay in between his arms and the sidewalk, as neighbors tried to console him. It's something I'll never forget—I learned during his moment of deepest pain that he was a recovering addict whose dogs were not only his therapeutic friends but his lifeline.

Since that moment, my dogs have NEVER been off-leash, unless in the confines of a home, dog park, yard, or office building that I know well, have researched, and approve of.

If you're going to own a dog, the time and effort that you put into training your dog is also time you spend training yourself in how to be a better pet owner. You will get that investment back in spades, because truly, your dog will live longer the better you treat it, and the safer its life is. In this chapter, you will learn how to react if you are attacked by a pet, what to do with your pet in any given situation, and how to train YOURSELF as much as the animal that you know and love.

BUT FIRST, YOU NEED TO KNOW . . .

Dognapping

How many reported cases are reported yearly?

▶ An estimated two million dogs in America are stolen every year . . . unfortunately, there's not trustworthy data for other types of pets.

▶ According to the American Kennel Club, "dog flipping" is a heartbreaking and criminal trend on the rise: A thief steals your dog, then sells it for a profit. This happens frequently, sadly, to dog breeds that are easy to grab and run with: French bulldogs, Chihuahuas, and small terriers.

What are the best ways to keep your dog safe from theft?

▶ Microchipping! Don't hesitate to make sure that you can find your dog under any circumstances. While this may seem invasive to you, your voiceless dog will thank you for it when you find him hungry and lost far from home, or you're able to lead police to his captor.

▶ It sounds obvious, but never leave your dog outside your home unattended. Even fenced backyards are easy targets for thieves.

What dog breeds bite or injure people the most?

▶ The definitive research on dangerous dogs made suggestions that are still pervasive in our society: a 1990s CDC study on which dogs sent the most people to the emergency room, and ultimately killed them. Dying from a dog is so incredibly rare, and the owners of these dogs tend to be utterly neglectful (if not downright abusive), so take these stats with a grain of salt. The CDC says as much, writing, "Targeting a specific breed may be unproductive; a more effective approach may be to target chronically irresponsible dog owners."

▶ Male, unneutered dogs are most likely to attack.

▶ Pit bulls, Rottweilers, and German shepherds were the most likely breeds to attack, according to the latest statisitics.

The CDC says it better than I ever could, so I'll let them have the last word here: "Dogs provide many health and social benefits. Most of the approximately fifty-five million dogs in the United States never bite or kill humans. However, the findings in this report indicate that [fatalities for dog attacks] continue to occur and most are preventable."

EXPERT INTERVIEW
Steve Diller

STEVE DILLER has been working with animals since early 1973. Steve's first professional position was working alongside many top board-certified and general practice veterinarians in Westchester County at County Animal Clinic in Yonkers, New York. Steve became a licensed veterinary technician in September 1983 and soon afterward began teaching at Mercy College in the veterinary technology department teaching courses in clinical laboratory technique, surgical nursing, and applied animal behavior. Steve later taught courses at the United States Canine Academy and Canine Behavioral Science Center.

Steve maintains his New York State license in veterinary technology. When he is not teaching his human students, Steve trains approximately two to three thousand dog/owner teams yearly. Steve has been qualified in New York State Supreme Court as an expert in dog bite incidents and has published numerous articles in various publications. Steve is the author of *Dogs and Their People, Choosing and Training the Best Dog For You*, published by Hyperion, and has appeared on national television many times.

How many years of experience do you have with dogs?

I've been in the animal field for forty-four years. I guess sometimes you pick something and sometimes it picks you. Even when I was a kid, I was the animal guy. I remember when I was in fifth grade a teacher said to me, "Listen, you know, you're a pretty good writer but do you think you could pick a different subject? You know maybe get away from dogs a little bit?" So I asked, "Well what do you want me to write about?" And he said, "How about sports?" So I wrote about racing greyhounds.

So that was that. I just grew up this way and I eventually became more and more focused in a formal education around raising and training dogs. My focus is working with dogs.

What are the best practices when you get a brand-new dog?

Well, bringing the dog into the house is a huge commitment. And at the end of the day, it's not as important where that dog comes from—interestingly it's more important about the nature of the individual dog and breed. We know that a dog's genetic code is associated with some inherent behaviors—now, that doesn't always pan out. Guide dogs are a good example—most of the guide dogs I know are labs. And they're pretty good at it. That doesn't mean all labs are good guide dogs. Just like we know that Labradors tend to be swimming dogs, right? But still, some Labs don't like swimming. You have Rottweilers that don't make good protection dogs. You have a random dog in a litter of dogs bred specifically for hunting that can't hunt. In the end it's about that individual.

The best thing that we can do as new dog owners is to bring the dog into the family knowing that it is an individual. There's a lot of talk today about how every dog is born a good dog, and then it's all on us to keep that going. I love that. Now, there are some dogs that should not be in families. You can work to train them, but I'd say that the average family doesn't have the time or resources to take on that kind of intensive training. If you have kids, ask yourself if you'd trust your potential dog to be alone with your children.

OK, so know your dog. What else?

Go slow. Give both your dog and your family really realistic expectations in terms of the time, and energy, and setback there will be in training your dog and getting to know your dog. Your dog is an animal, not a computer program, and you can't always just do the work in the prescribed number of training sessions and expect that your dog will absorb all the material and act accordingly.

To go back to before you even choose or bring home a dog— do your research. Yes, you need to research behavior, but you also need to research how much your vet bills will be for a broken limb or a severe illness. These costs can vary widely based on your neighborhood and the breed of your dog and the size of your dog. You need to research the ongoing cost of food that your particular kind of dog would need, and any equipment and grooming that they need. Some people even buy health insurance for their pets, which is a cost you'd also need to factor into your budget. There may be liabilities for you and your family in taking in a dog—especially a dog that's older with a history of biting or aggressive behavior. Not all rescue shelter dogs come with accurate records of past behavior—especially if it was rescued as a stray.

On top of costs, your dog also needs a substantial amount of your time. On the top of that list of obligations is exercise. Consider the frequency and length of walks your dog would need each day, and ask yourself if you can realistically give that. Otherwise, it's not fair to the dog for you to adopt it. Once exercise has been factored in, as a potential pet owner, you need to assume that behavioral issues in your dog will arise. Do you have the time, money, and emotional energy to deal with an unstable animal? The behavioral issues could be your fault, or they could be the fault of the dog's genetics, or the issues could be coming from a combination of both of those things. Maybe you've lived with the dog for three years and things were going great—until they weren't. It's not good for anyone—you or the dog—to deny that poor, and potentially dangerous, behavior is taking place. Aggressive or even simply irritating behaviors in dogs can be fixed if they are addressed early.

What's the number one thing you see dog owners doing wrong?
Some owners do not expose the dog to the wide range of interactions and environments that they're going to be in throughout their lives, while they are in the short time span you could call the dog's "learning period." We see more and more that a door closes, so to speak, at eighteen weeks old. The opportunity for ideal socialization slams shut—that's it. You can't go get a six-month-old dog that's been isolated up until the time you adopt it and expect it to get along perfectly with your family and friends. There's chemistry that's taking place in the dog's neural pathways, where ideally, you'd start exposing it to every person and every situation it could encounter starting at eight weeks old.

I recommend taking a puppy home at eight weeks old and exposing it to most things it could encounter by twelve weeks old—that gives you the best shot at having a well-adjusted, social, friendly dog. In my experience, more than training the dog to sit, and come, and lie down (which is what people hire me for), your dog's social process is the most important training to check off the list.

There was a time that veterinarians suggested that if a dog is not fully vaccinated, it shouldn't be going out. So, you still have families keeping a puppy in the house or on their property and not exposed to real life until after his final vaccine, which usually comes around that the sixteen- to eighteen-week mark—and then you're going to start exposing your dog to new things, and you're probably going to run into some social issues.

Now, some dogs just come out of the factory, so to speak, with really strong nerve thresholds. Nothing bothers them. You can cuddle some dogs when they're sleeping and they'll love it, or you can drop a pen next to some dogs and they'll start barking. If you don't socialize your dog well, you run the very real risk that it's going to end up in a shelter at some point, unless you're really willing to manage that dog for the rest of its life. That's the big deal.

For years now, the American Veterinary Medical Association has recommended to the veterinary to tell their clients to have their puppies formally socialized before twelve weeks. But that advice just doesn't seem to filter out to your average veterinarian. A lot of these guys are sticking with fifty-year-old advice, which is based on a time when America had not only a lot of very sick dogs, but a lot of stray dogs. Back then, it actually was dangerous to have a family pet interacting with anything and everything before it was fully vaccinated. But the truth is, we're just not finding that to be the case anymore. I live in New York, and it's rare to see a dog out and about that's sick, and it's perhaps equally rare that you see a dog without an owner at the dog park.

Steve Diller's first professional position was working alongside many top board-certified and general practice veterinarians in Westchester County at County Animal Clinic in Yonkers, New York.

■■■■■■■■■■■

EXPERT INTERVIEW
Officer Ted Dahlin

We know you have experience with trained police dogs in the field, and that's affected how you feel about dogs. What can a dog owner do to keep them safe and healthy?

No matter your dog's role, treat your dog like a partner, not an object. For some American dog owners, depending on your profession, a dog is both a partner and a tool. And if you don't take care of a tool, it's not going to work when you need it. I know most people don't use their dogs for anything other than companionship, but no matter the dog's role, taking care of basic needs goes a very long way. Dogs are amazing creatures—they don't expect much other than food and some affection, and they will become your best friend.

What else can make the dog's life and the owner's life easier?

Obedience is key, whether it's a law enforcement dog or a pet. If your dog is obedient, you can do anything together. A key component of obedience is the dog knowing its rank—remember, it's a partner, but it's not an equal partner. Dogs are animals first, not humans, and they are pack animals, and packs have ranks.

Give dogs a purpose, give them something to do, and they will be happy and, quite possibly, they won't lash out.

Don't be afraid of putting your dog in a crate if you're going out for a few hours. I know dogs are our babies, but what's worse—keeping them in a crate for an hour or two, or letting them get into a chemical substance in the house that you didn't store properly, and then they suffer illness? Or they run around and a piece of furniture or a heavy object falls on them? Take responsibility and secure both household items and your pets.

We've all seen it—dogs open doors, they jump up on counters, they do crazy, crazy things that you wouldn't think they could to get something that they want. Remember, dogs have a sense of smell that's fifty times better than ours. If something smells good to them, they're going to want to check it out. I think, err on the side of always securing potentially dangerous items and always securing the dog if you can't be there to look after it.

It all comes down to paying attention.

What about walking your dog?

My vote is to keep them on a leash. You have control. Protect your dog. Take control, be dominant, and the aggressive dog might back down. It's extremely, extremely difficult to break up a fight between two dogs, so try to stop it before it starts. Pay attention to your surroundings as you're walking your dog. Is there an open gate or an open door in your line of sight? Assume a dog could come running out of it. Maybe move to the other side of the street, or put yourself between the dog and the potential danger.

Now let's look at cars. There's a fine line between cute and dangerous, especially when a dog is sitting in your lap. Think about your kids—you've got them in a seat belt or a car seat in the back seat—so aim for something like a crate in the back seat.

What should we avoid with our dogs at all costs?

Never give your dog cooked bones, which can fragment into hundreds of extremely sharp pieces. I'd avoid table scraps altogether.

Officer Dahlin has worked in law enforcement since October 1998, adding a primary focus on K-9s to the mix in 2006. He boasts over three thousand hours of training in law enforcement and K-9s. He earned the Texas Award for Valor in 2013 from the Texas Commission on Law Enforcement. Today, Ted is a deputy at the Harris County Sheriff's Office near Houston, Texas.

EXPERT INTERVIEW

Dr. Richard Jakimer

For dog and cat owners, what items, if ingested, need to set off
loud alarm bells and immediate responses?

One of the most frequent issues I see in my office is animals in-
gesting food or objects around the house that we wouldn't think
might be toxic, but they are. Chocolate is a big one, because of the
caffeine-related chemicals that animals like dogs and cats cannot
digest. Another one is grapes—research suggests there's a com-
pound in grapes that can affect the kidneys in a lot of dogs.

Another substance to avoid near your pets is a sweetener called
xylitol, which is found in a lot of gums. It's highly toxic in some
mammals because it can cause low blood sugar very quickly and
it can create liver failure very, very quickly with a relatively small
amount. And don't forget acne and skin creams—dogs and cats
can bite into tubes and quickly absorb into their systems chemicals that are highly toxic.

Houseplants are another item that I highly recommend keeping
out of pets' reach. In many cases, the leaves (which dogs and
cats especially love to chew on) are either toxic or sharp, and cut
the mouth or esophagus. So before you bring home a new pet,
consider moving or getting rid of some plants. Cats especially love
fibrous leaves and string. During the holidays, we see cats ingest
wrapping ribbons often, which can ultimately block or cut the cat's
intestines. I've actually needed to remove a foot of intestines
from a cat who ate string that destroyed its digestive system. This
particular story ended well—the cat actually gained weight and had
a great life once it could eat again—but something as simple as
leaving around Christmas wrapping could lead to your pet's injury.

Here are some other items that you might not ever have considered but can look appealing to our pets: river rocks in plants, glass stones, bingo chips, broken glass (which looks like ice to them—yum!), coins, bottle caps. Again, holiday season traps: Cats can drink the water you put in the base of your Christmas tree, which has leeched toxic chemicals from the evergreen.

Let's say you know your dog or cat has ingested one of those items, or something similar. What should you do?

You should try to induce vomiting. You can do that relatively simply by getting some hydrogen peroxide. On a smaller dog, use a teaspoon; for a larger dog, a tablespoon or two. Hold their the head level and pour that into the mouth. Hydrogen peroxide foams in the stomach, makes them nauseous, and they vomit.

The rule of thumb is that if they don't vomit after the first fifteen minutes, do it again, and then again after that. In any case, you should also be consulting with and possibly working on getting your pet to a veterinarian. This is especially true if you come home to your pet after you've been away for a few hours and you suspect they've ingested something toxic, because the toxin might have moved through the stomach already, and you're beyond the point of having vomiting help. So work to induce vomiting, but also get in touch with your vet.

All the more reason to get in touch with your vet immediately: Some toxins should not be expelled by vomiting—because that could make matters worse. Some of those items are any cleansing agents. We know that these substances have a bitter taste or just plain horrible taste, so it's unlikely that your pet would ingest any large amount. Not inducing vomiting is also true if the item could be sharp—this could cause more harm than good coming up through the esophagus. For that reason alone, dogs and cats should never eat chicken bones, which are exceptionally sharp.

But again—call your vet! Your pet's life could be on the line.

Let's say your dog has been cut or bruised. What should a pet owner do in that case?

Try to secure the dog so that it can't bite you. No matter how much you love each other, it is a fact that the natural instinct for any animal is to go into protective drive, biting or lashing out at anything or anyone it thinks could touch that spot. When they feel pain, they react out of instinct, not training. So restrain the animal so that they don't end up nipping into you. After restraining, the first thing you want to do is apply direct pressure and wrap the wound tightly, and get to a veterinary emergency clinic immediately. Dog's arteries especially are highly pressurized, so a relatively small cut could surprise you with how much bleeding can result.

What's your key piece of advice for someone bringing home a new cat or a new dog, especially if it's a kitten or a puppy?

One piece of advice would be to isolate the puppy or the kitten in a small room like a bathroom, with nothing that it can chew up; isolate electric cords, which can be extremely dangerous. Do this until you can observe that animal and know that it knows its boundaries—like it's not jumping up, getting on the shelves, knocking down pottery and glass objects. We're not worried about the objects breaking, but we are worried about the new pet jumping down from the shelf and gashing its paw on shattered glass.

For nearly forty years, Dr. Jakimer has run one of the most prestigious veterinary clinics in Westchester County, New York. He completed his veterinary internship and residency program at the Animal Medical Center in New York City after graduating from Kansas State University. Today, his focus is the safety and health of the cats and dogs he continues to treat daily at Manor Veterinary Clinic.

CHAPTER FOURTEEN

Looking Forward

The Future of Safety and Security

I SEE MY CLOSING this book and your closing this book as both an ending and a beginning. But before I look to the future, I'd like to revisit the past—we all know that since man inhabited caves, we've always wanted to protect our stuff.

Starting with the earliest humans, I'd imagine their early form of an alarm system could have been a crude trip-wire system of branches and leaves. Later on, as our technological know-how accelerated, mankind created weapons, domesticated dogs, and amplified fortifications to protect themselves—from drawbridges, to moats, and to all those other nasty, gory medieval anti-intruder contraptions we see in movies—but the human intent remains the same: How can I stay alive, and keep who I love and what I love safe?

Today, locks, doors, bars, and windows are becoming stronger and smaller, even as I write this. Today, we have wireless motion detection and hidden cameras—even some that capture and identify faces and license plates. Tomorrow promises even more advances, and some that make my head shake, especially as we enter into an age where biometrics, predictive behavior aids, and tracking technology will be available to the common civilian. Formidable stuff indeed.

Now that you're feeling oh so safe, let me scare you a bit. For every action taken by the safety, security, and home protection community, there's a REACTION from bad actors. We are engaged in a never-ending arms race between keeping our homes and bodies safe, and the know-how of those who are intent on committing you harm.

Giving credence to the saying "the more things change, the more they stay the same" (never more so than here), we have so much in common with early families, Renaissance single women, prehistoric pets, World War I gun owners, and past-century counterterrorism experts. For all the advancements in safety and security, in my opinion, NOTHING will keep you from harm as much as you, your knowledge, and your reactions! The fear and anxiety of living a human life has been with us since the beginning . . . but how are we preparing?

We prepare by practicing. We commit to keeping up with our safety and security education, practicing and enhancing our situational awareness and critical and strategic thinking, and knowing that our mind is our best defense against becoming a statistic. After reading this book and putting its recommendations into your daily routine and your daily thought process, you will face the world, and all its dangers (and its joys), moving through life Prepared, Not Scared.

ACKNOWLEDGMENTS

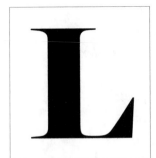

ET ME first thank my publisher, but more importantly my friend David Zinczenko, for his faith, confidence, and patience in me to get this done.

It's also important to know that the contributors all were so kind to add their expertise and wisdom. This book could not have been written without them or the collective love, knowledge, patience, and support of the following people. You have my most sincere gratitude.

Terry (Mom) and Matthew (Bro) Stanton

Brad and Lamia Jacobs and Family

Jay Novik

John, KK, Sinclair and Schiller Ranch

Big Al Sessa

Sly and Jennifer Stallone

Bill Bratton and Rikki Klieman, Esq.

Megyn Kelly, Esq., and Doug Brunt

Marilyn Chinitz, Esq., and Family

John Herzfeld and Rebekah Chaney

Phil Houston and the QVerity Team

Shirine Coburn and Coburn Communications

The Fitzgerald Family

David Zinczenko and Shana Wall

Bob and Lillian Wall

Dan Abrams, Esq.

Stephen Lang

Robert (Bob) Conrad

Lara Spencer

Kimberly Guilfoyle, Esq.

Dr. Raja Flores

Dr. Jane Fitzgerald and Family Chiropractic

Dr. Emilio Biagiotti

Dr. Steve Pearlman

Mark Speranza

Rachel Stockman, Esq.

Jon and Brandis Dietelbaum

Al and Donna Parlato and Family

Robert Strent, Esq.

Larry Shire, Esq.

Rich Gaspari

Tom Ruskin

Robert Sharenow

Frank Shea

Marc Victor

Kevin Reily

Pat Rogers (RIP)

Bill Lappe

Chief Steve Silks

Chief Tom Fahey

Chief Russell Green

Noah Oppenheim

Joe Tacopina, Esq.

Dr. Jeff Dorfman and Family

Jerry Mussano and Family

Al Ginetti and Family

Frank and Barbara Hoffman

Stephanie Levinson

Steve, Rafael, Jim, and Erik

Eric Handler

Tara Lane of G &D's

Victoria Gotti

Michael Freidson

Dan Magnan

Deputy PC John Miller

Ira Rosen

Paul Pietropaulo

Brian Kilmeade

Neal P. Cavuto

Andrew Wilkow, Wilkow Majority

Matt Zimmerman

Chris Cuomo, Esq.

Joey Bilancia

Joe Heroun

Santina Lucci

Chris Viasto

"FORGE"

Alliance Tactical Training
and Facility

Dr. Mehmet Oz and Show Team

Dr. Drew Pinsky

Rachael Ray and Show Team

Bill Breen

Mike Swain

Craig Horowitz

Bob Read and Inside Edition Team

Joe Weyer

Bishop and Lucy Stanton

CICA and City Island Residents

Deborah Norville

Rocky, Alexa and Abby

Brady Family

Michael and Karin Barrett

Lou Palombo

Insp. Carlos Ghonz

Jonathan T. Gilliam

Rosanna Scotto

Josh Morgan

Eric Zinczenko

Richard Emery, Esq.

Steven Brown

M.K. Metzger

John and Barbara Neuner

Trish R.

Wayne and Fran Genovese

Tom and Bob Forcelli

K9s4Cops and K9s4Kids

Shelly Watts Cross

Kingshepherd.com

Mark Gjonaj

Frank Carone, Esq.

Howard Fensterman, Esq.

Lynne Smith

Teddy Pryor, Esq.

Joy Behar

Barbara Fedida

Judith Regan

Jay Glazer

Sarah Derham

Larry Hutcher, Esq.

Leslie Barbara, Esq.

Kevin McKlean

Joe Rogen

Terry George

Jeff Csatari

Steven Van Zandt

Charleen and Kenny Sachs, Esq.

Craig Jacobson

Billy Bildstein

CRN Digital Talk

The Doctors

James and Annik Grage

The PIRI Family

Dr. Eric Berg

Kenny Schrachter

John and Lee Raimondi

Rob Lee

Gary Benz

The View